# CROCHET AFGHANS

## Discover How to Crochet a Perfect Afghan in Less Than a Day

By Emma Brown

Copyright© 2015 by Emma Brown - All rights reserved. Printed in the United States of America.

**Copyright**: No part of this publication may be reproduced without written permission from the author, except by a reviewer who may quote brief passages or reproduce illustrations in a review with appropriate credits; nor may any part of this book be reproduced, stored in a retrieval system, or transmitted in any form or by any means – electronic, mechanical, photocopying, recording, or other - without prior written permission of the copyright holder.

The trademarks are used without any consent, and the publication of the trademark is without permission or backing by the trademark owner. All trademarks and brands within this book are for clarifying purposes only and are owned by the owners themselves.

First Printing, 2015 - Printed in the United States of America

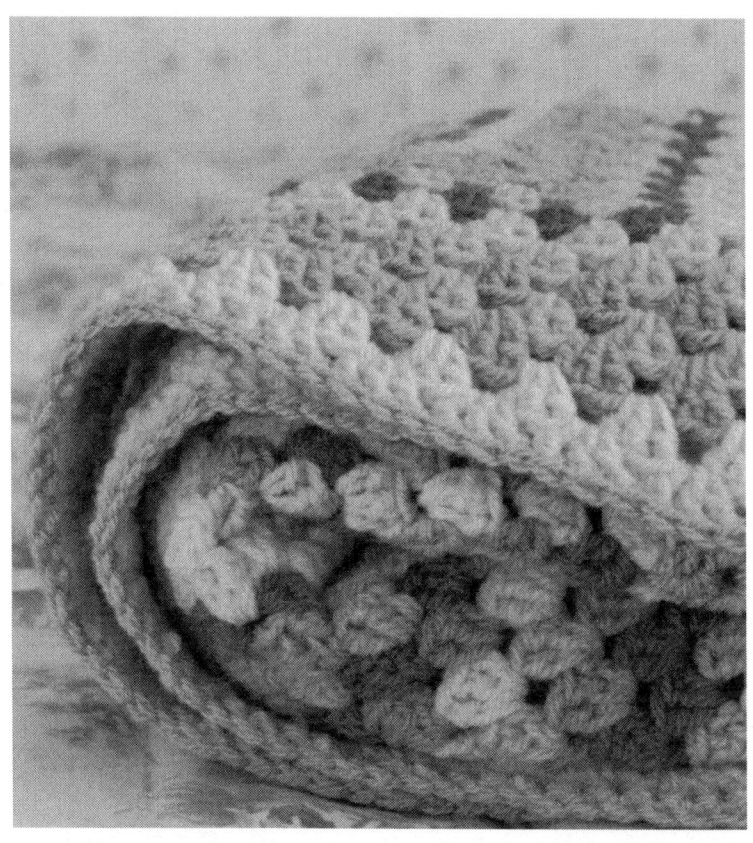

*"My mother taught me many craft and household skills but she never taught me to crochet. For that I have to thank her, as it meant I had to teach myself"*

# TABLE OF CONTENTS

| | |
|---|---|
| Introduction | 1 |
| Crocheting Afghans | 3 |
| Tools and Materials | 9 |
|     Hooks | 10 |
|     Yarns | 16 |
|     Choosing Hooks and Yarn for your Project | 20 |
|     Other Equipment | 25 |
| Understanding Patterns | 27 |
|     Crochet Terminology | 29 |
| Crochet Pattern Basics | 31 |
|     Starting a Crochet Pattern | 30 |
|     Finishing Project | 41 |
| Basic Stitches | 43 |
| Techniques | 53 |
| Advanced Stitches | 65 |
| Crocheting Tips | 75 |
| Afghan Patterns | 79 |

| | |
|---|---|
| Beginner | 80 |
| Intermediate | 131 |
| Advanced | 242 |
| Glossary | 245 |
| FAQ | 249 |
| Conclusion | 253 |
| About the Author | 255 |

# INTRODUCTION

Crocheting is a hobby that is increasing in popularity and this is for a wide range of reasons. Not only is it fun to create your own clothing, toys and home wares, and a brilliant way to express your creativity, it is also relaxing, entertaining and often it creates a strong bond with friends or family if you decide to collaborate on a project. Afghans are a great project that can be completed alone or in a team – either way is fun!

**This guide is designed to give you all of the tools you need to complete a crochet afghan pattern in less than a day.** What better way could you spend your time? Within the chapters below, **you will find all the details on every stitch, every technique and everything you need to know** – so even if you are a complete beginner, you will have all the information you need at your fingertips. The step-by-step guides will ensure that none of the information given in an afghan crochet pattern will confuse you.

*Crochet* is derived from the French word meaning '*hook*' and it's the process of creating fabric from yarn, thread or other material strands using a *crochet hook*. These hooks can be made from *metals*, *woods* or *plastic*. The process of crocheting is very similar to that of knitting, in that it consists of pulling loops of material through other loops. It differs from knitting however because only one stitch is active at a time, and the hook is used rather than knitting needles, which creates a wide range of unique stitches allowing you to create some very special products. Many people find crocheting easier to master as it only uses one primary tool, but this simplicity allows you to become much more creative with your designs.

# CROCHETING AFGHANS

***Afghans*** are a fun and simplistic project that can be completed with even the most basic of knowledge of crochet. They use the very simple, *single crochet stitch* and *double crochet stitch* – all of which are easy to master – and can be coordinated to suit your personal needs. If you choose to include more complex stitches into your design, you can. Some people prefer one solid color, other prefer stripes…the beauty of this pattern is that you can make it whatever you want, and it's so easy to make that you can combine the activity with something else; watching television, listening to the radio, talking to your friends, etc.

As **afghans are an uncomplicated square or rectangle shape**, you can adapt any pattern to ensure that the product you create is a size that suits you.

***There are three basic sizes that will usually be included:***

**Afghan** – 50" by 65" (127cm by 165cm)

**Lap Blanket** – 35" by 40" (89cm by 101cm)

**Baby Blanket** – 25" by 30" (63cm by 76cm)

But of course, these are just for guidance. The more you practice crocheting afghans, the easier it will become for you to adapt a pattern – or even create your own.

As a guideline, ***the following sizes are generally used, depending on who the afghan is for:***

**Preemie** – 15" (38cm) square

**Baby** – 30" – 36" (76cm – 91cm)

**Children** – 42" (107cm) by whatever length is necessary according to their age. The standard bed size is 75" (190cm)

**Adult** – 48" by 75" (122cm by 190cm) (but add extra width if necessary).

You may of course choose to **afghan in squares** which adds a new set of dimensions to it. You will need to ensure that each square is equal in size and work out the size you want accordingly.

Below is a ***guide for how many squares you will need to create an afghan at your chosen size:***

# CROCHET AFGHANS

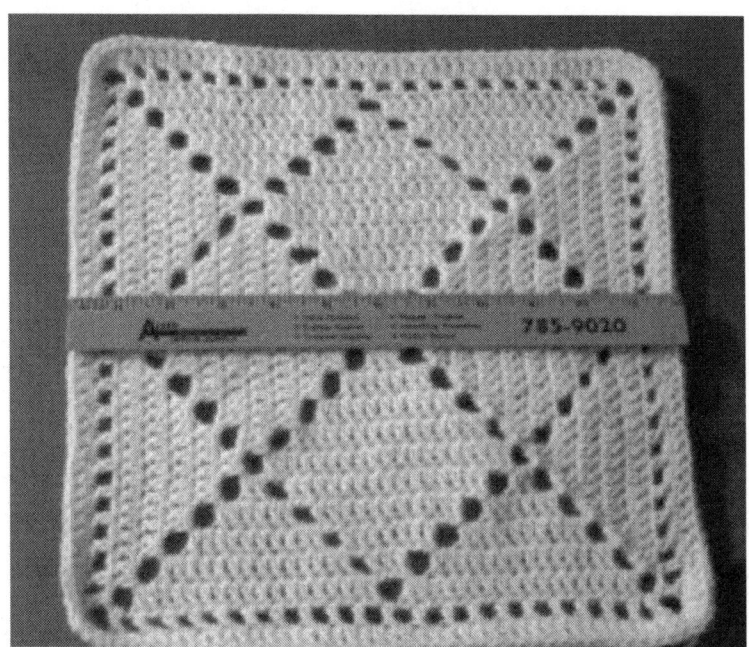

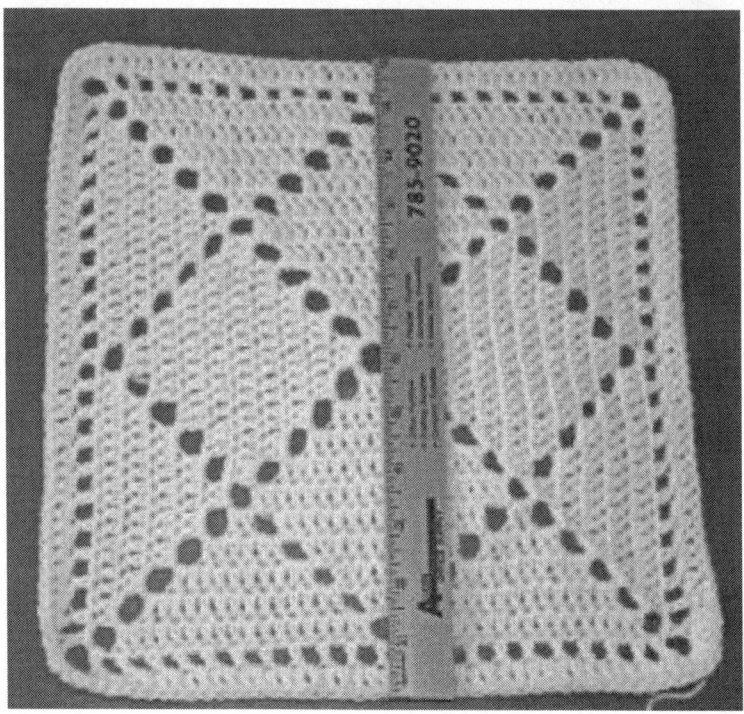

## EMMA BROWN

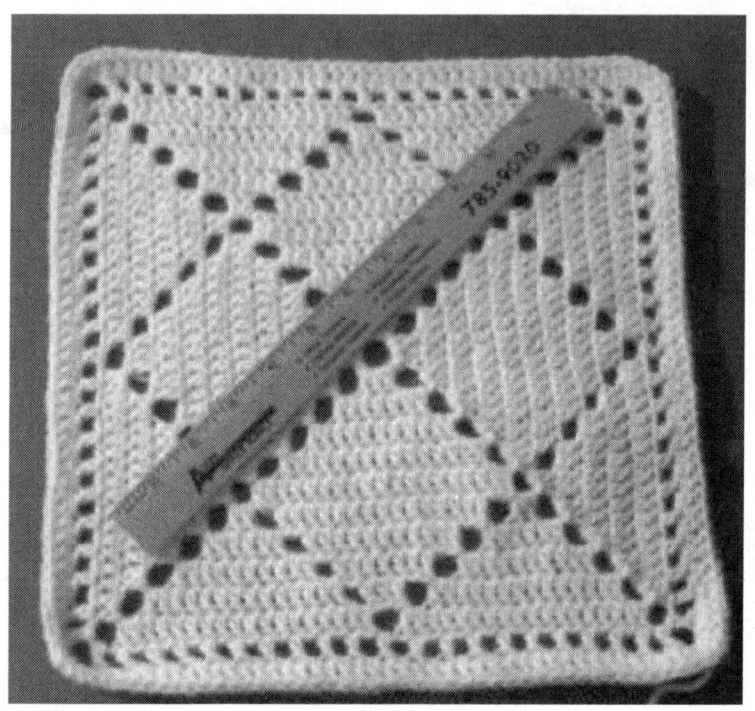

CROCHET AFGHANS

# Mattress Size

***Bassinet***: 19-24" (48-61cm) x 33-38" (84-96cm) **Using 6" (15cm) squares:** For a preemie, try 3 x 5. For a full term baby, it is better to go a little bigger.

***Jenny Lind Cradle***: 39 x 22" (99 x 56cm). 75 inch x 34.5 inches (190 x 88cm) **Using 6" squares:** 7 x 4

***Crib***: 28 x 52" (71 x 132cm) **Using 6" squares:** 5 x 8

Baby Afghans should make use of fine yarn to craft it lighter.

***Twin***: 39 inch x 75 inch (99 x 190cm) **Using 6" squares:** 6 x 12 inch, 7 x 13 inch, 7 x 14 inch

***King***: 78" x 80" (198 x 203cm) **Using 6" squares:** 13 x 14 **Using 9" (23cm) squares:** 9 x 9 **Using 12" (30cm) squares:** 7 x 7

# Blanket Size

***Twin:*** 66 inch x 90 inch (167 x 228cm) **Using 6 inch squares:** 11 x 15 create it 66" x 90" plus binding **Using 9inch squares:** 7 x 10 create it 63" x 90" x plus binding.

***King:*** 108" x 90" (274 x 228 cm) **Using 6 inch squares:** 18 x 15 create it 108 inch x 90 inch plus binding.

# TOOLS AND MATERIALS

There is a selection of equipment that you'll need for starting any crochet project, including an afghan. The pattern will often give you some details on what you need, but it is a good idea to have some knowledge on what is available.

# Hooks

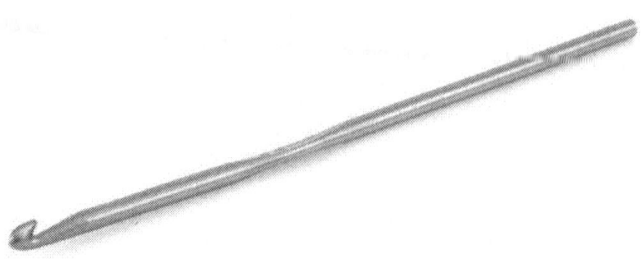

The hook (sometimes referred to as the crochet needle) is the most important tool when starting a crocheting project. **It's a tool with a hook on one end that is used to draw yarn or thread through knotted loops.** Only one is needed to create any crochet stitch.

Crochet hooks are typically made of wood, plastic, metal or casein. They are designed for right or left-handed use and the handles are all shaped in different ways for comfort, ease-of-use or personal preference.

**There are two ways to hold a crochet hook:**

**The Pencil Grip** – which involves holding the hook in the same way you would hold a pencil.

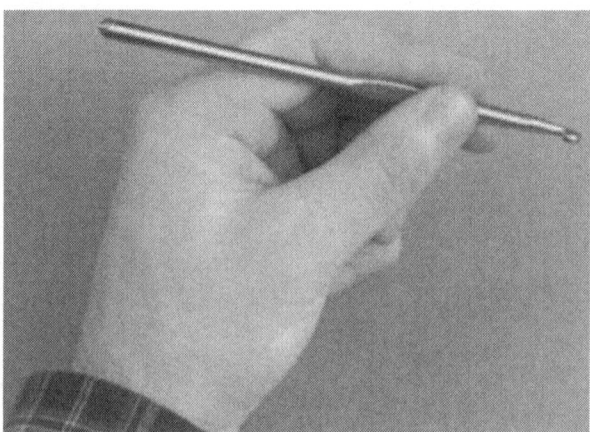

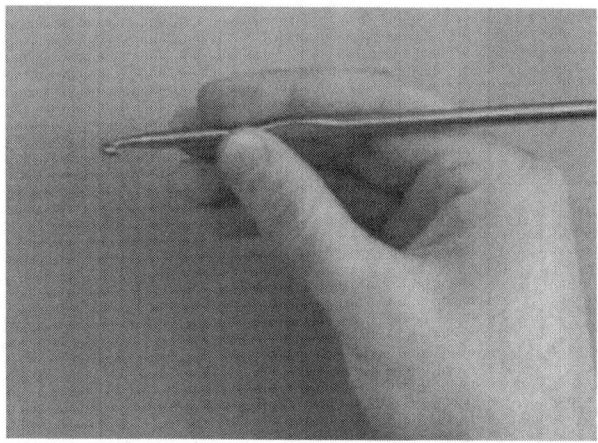

*The Knife Grip* – which is holding the hook in an overhang grip, in a similar way to how you would hold a knife.

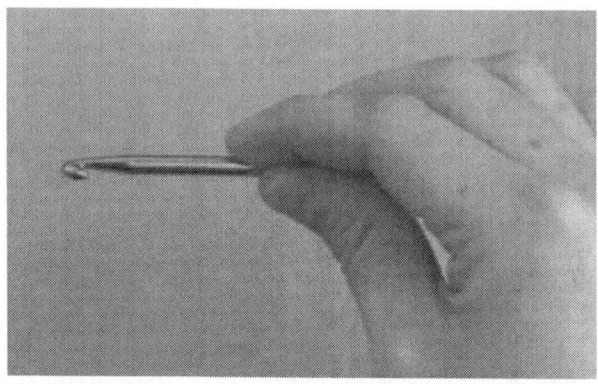

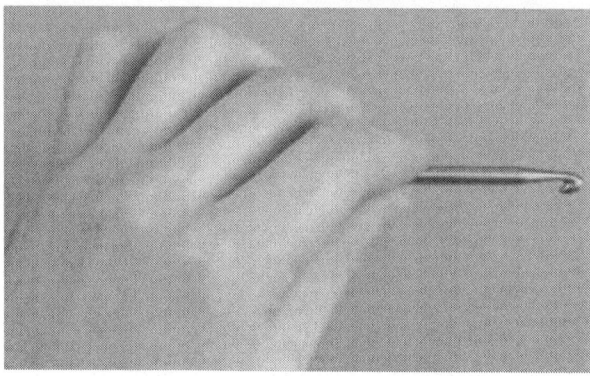

The way you should hold the hook depends on what is the most comfortable for you. Some people like to switch between the holds to prevent hand cramp or weariness.

It's essential that you select the right crochet hook, not only for the yarn you have selected and the project you're working on, but also for your comfort. Working with the right hook will make all the difference to your finished project.

Below is a **guide to the types of hooks available**.

***Inline vs. Not Inline*** – Although the visual difference between an inline and not-inline hook is very subtle, the impact it will have on your crocheting is not. The notch on an inline hook is more passive, as it is all along one single line. If the hook has any overhang, it is referred to as not inline. Whichever hook you choose, depends on your personal preference.

*Inline*

*Not Inline*

**The hook is made up of many different parts**, all of which play a very important role to the crochet project. **They are as follows**:

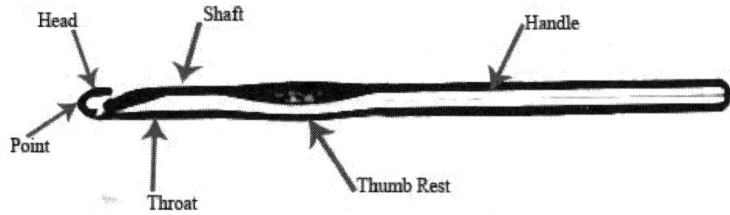

*Head* – the head of the hook is where the yarn is kept.

*Shaft* – this is the neck of the hook, which is either shaped inline or not inline.

*Handle* – this is the portion of the hook held by the crochetier.

*Thumb Rest* – this is where you rest your thumb for comfort.

*Throat* – this is the gap which holds the yarn.

*Point* – this is the very tip of the hook that is pushed into the loops of yarn.

These factors all vary in the different types of crochet hooks, and the decision on which hook(s) you purchase depends on what you'll be using the tool for.

**Below are a few examples of what is currently on the market** (shown from left to right in the image below):

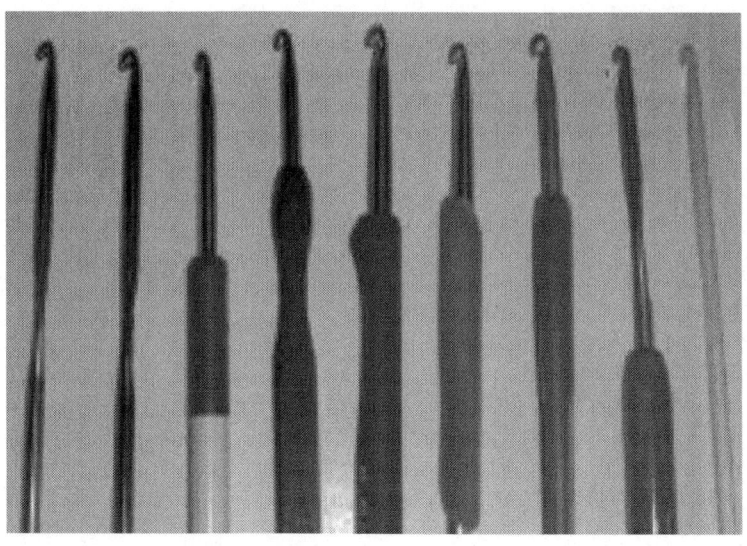

**Generic Aluminum Hook** – these hooks are generally not inline and cheap, which can be problematic if you need something sturdy. Always consider thickness when buying one of these.

**Boye Hook** – these hooks are also not inline, and are the most commonly referred to when talking about styles. They are very popular; most people who love to crochet have a selection in different sizes.

**Addi Comfort Grip Hook** – these hooks are designed with comfort in mind. The shorter handle means less to work with. Addi is a European manufacturer so their products are typically found online.

**Kollage Square Hook** – these are rounded, not inline hooks which are aimed at people who prefer to work with the hook in the knife grip. Kollage is American made and available in a range of different sizes and shapes.

**Tulip Etimo Hook**– these hooks are manufactured in Japan and are sturdy, sitting in between inline and not inline, making them the best of both worlds. They are more suitable for pencil grip users.

**Hamanaka Raku Rake Double-Ended Hook** – these hooks are also manufactured in Japan. The double-ended, shorter hooks are comfortable in both styles of hold.

**Clover Soft Touch Hook** – the head of these hooks is in between inline and not inline. It's sturdy and comfortable to use with a range of materials.

**Susan Bates Hook** – these are inline hooks with are a great alterative to Boye. They're inexpensive and work well.

**Bamboo Hook** – these hooks are inline with a cylindrical shaped handle. They are shorter which some prefer, but others find more challenging to work with. The usage of this depends on your grip, and is better tested before buying.

*The Craft Yarn Council of America* – an industry trade association – has formulated a **standard crochet hook and knitting needle sizes**. The crochet hook size is measured by the thickness of the shaft.

## CROCHET AFGHANS

| Millimeter Range | Crochet Hook Size (Numerical) | Crochet Hook Size (Letter) |
| --- | --- | --- |
| 2.25mm | 1 | B |
| 2.75mm | 2 | C |
| 3.25mm | 3 | D |
| 3.5mm | 4 | E |
| 3.75mm | 5 | F |
| 4mm | 6 | G |
| 4.5mm | 7 | - |
| 5mm | 8 | H |
| 5.5mm | 9 | I |
| 6mm | 10 | J |
| 6.5mm | 10.5 | K |
| 8mm | 11 | L |
| 9mm | 13 | M |
| 10mm | 15 | N |
| 11.5mm | 16 | P |
| 15mm | 19 | P/Q |
| 16mm | - | Q |
| 19mm | 35 | S |
| 25mm | 50 | - |

# Yarns

The yarn is what you'll be using to create your afghan, so you will want to choose one that you like, but also one that is suitable for the equipment you have and the project you're working on.

**When buying the yarn, there are a few things you should take into consideration:**

*Yarn Texture* – smooth yarn is easier to work with for a first project.

*Yarn Color* – lighter colors are easier to work with as you can see the stitches better.

*Yarn vs. Crochet Thread* – thread is more challenging to work with, but perfect for projects such as doilies.

*Yarn Weights* – Medium to higher weights are easier to start with.

On top of this, when creating an afghan you might also want to consider; *novelty vs. plain*, *fiber*, *quality*, and *amount*. *Color* is something that will impact on the appearance of your afghan greatly, so combine colors that will look good together and chose something that will suit the rest of your – or whoever the gift is for – home.

### The main choices of yarn available are:

***Wool Yarn*** – this is an excellent choice for practicing crochet stitches as it's easy to unravel and rework.

***Cotton Yarn*** – this is an inelastic fiber which makes it slightly more challenging than wool.

***Acrylic Yarn*** – this is very popular as it's available in a variety of colors and it's also affordable.

**The way you hold the yarn** while you work is down to what feels comfortable for you, but below are a few tips to get you started:

- You place the yarn in your less dominant hand.

- The yarn hand feeds the yarn to your hook.

- The yarn hand controls the tension of the yarn being fed, and determines how loose or tight your finished project will be.

- You can practice weaving the yarn through your fingers to see which feels the most comfortable and controlled for you.

The *Craft Council of America* has produced a **chart of yarn weights and their suitability to crochet hooks**:

# CROCHET AFGHANS

| Yarn Weight: | 0 Lace | 1 Super | 2 Fine | 3 Light | 4 Medium | 5 Bulk | 6 Super |
|---|---|---|---|---|---|---|---|
| Types of Yarn in Category. | Thread, Cobweb, Lace | Sock, Baby. | Sport, Baby | DK, Light, Worsted. | Worsted, Afghan. | Chunky, Craft, Rug. | Bulky, Roving. |
| Knit Gauge Range in Stockinet Stich to 4 inches. | 30 – 40 sts | 27 – 32 sts | 23 – 26 sts | 21 – 24 sts | 16 – 20 sts | 12 – 15 sts | 6 – 11 sts |
| Recommended Needle in Metric Size Range. | 1.5 – 2.25mm | 2.25 – 3.25mm | 3.25 – 3.75mm | 3.75 – 4.5mm | 4.5 – 5.5mm | 5.5 – 8mm | 8mm and larger |
| Recommended Needle in US Size Range. | 000 – 1 | 1 – 3 | 3 – 5 | 5 – 7 | 7 – 9 | 9 – 11 | 11 and more |
| Crochet Gauge Range in Single Crochet to 4 inch. | 32 – 42 double crochets | 21 – 32 sts | 16 – 20 sts | 12 – 17 sts | 11 – 14 sts | 8 – 11 sts | 5 – 9 Sts |
| Recommended Hook in Metric Size Range. | Steel 1.6 – 1.4mm | 2.25 – 3.5mm | 3.5 – 4.5mm | 4.5 – 5.5mm | 5.5 – 6.5mm | 6.5 – 9mm | 9mm and larger |
| Recommended Hook in US Size Range. | Steel 6, 7, 8 Regular Hook b-1 | B-1 to E-9 | E-4 to 7 | 7 to I-9 | I-9 to K10½ | K10½ to M-13 | M13 and larger |

# Choosing Hooks And Yarn For Your Project

**Lace (Cobweb)**

This is thinnest sort of yarn and just a slightly thicker than thread; it is best for doilies and lace making.

*Hook*: Steel 6-8 and Regular B

**Fingering**

It's extremely thin as well. It's best for socks and lace projects.

*Hook*: B-E

**Sport**

It's very fine and impeccable for making baby blankets and clothes. It can be knit up to as thin as a cardigan.

*Hook*: E-7

### Light Worsted

It's known as "D K" it is smooth or even-textured.

*Hook*: 7-I

### Worsted

It is thicker and often utilized for sweaters and blankets.

*Hook*: I-K

**Chunky**

It's really thick and often utilized for rugs and scarves. It's bulky and creates interesting effect.

*Hook*: K-M

**Roving**

It's unspun wool often utilized for felting.

*Hook*: M and Up

**Varying Thickness**

# CROCHET AFGHANS

Yarn may also change it in thickness with a strand, by give a bumpy and uneven materials.

## Heathered or Tweed

It's placed flecks of different shades' fiber randomly.

## Ombre

It is a variegated colored, which fades from light to dark shades of the similar hue.

## Multi-colored

It's variegated along two or above diverse colors.

## Self-striping

It is dyed with particular lengths of two colors. It creates stripes, when knitted.

## Shimmer

To add some sparkling flecks of tinsel are added in it.

# Other Equipment

*For your afghan crochet pattern, you will also need:*

***Scissors*** – A small pair of blunt-end scissors in good condition is preferred.

***T-Pins*** – Which is used for blocking and securing pieces of project together when joining or measuring.

***Yarn Needle*** – Made of plastic or metal with a blunt point and large eye. It is used to hide loose ends when joining yarn or when project is finished.

***Tape Measure*** – Normally it is used to measure length and width of project.

***Gauge Ruler*** – A 2-inch L shaped window item that allows you to measure the number of stitches and rows in an inch.

***Split Markers*** – Round plastic spiral markers that slip into crochet work. They are used to indicate a certain point in crocheting like joining continuous rounds, enlarge points or reduce points.

***Notebook*** – Useful to help you keep track of what row or round you are crocheting and the number of times you have repeated stitches.

***Container*** – Anything will do to hold your hooks, scissors, and yarn needles and other equipment.

# UNDERSTANDING PATTERNS

A key part to reading **crochet patterns** is understanding the language they are written in. They **use a lot of abbreviations** to make the text more concise. These abbreviations are included in the Glossary section of this guide.

Once you are familiar with abbreviations, you will need to work out if the pattern is written in *rows* or *rounds*. **Rows** will be to create something back and forth, such as a blanket; **rounds** are to crate tubes with no seams, such as for a hat.

In the pattern, the directions for each round or row will be written on a separate line. **If you're working in rows**, you'll turn your work at the end of each row then work back across the top of the previous row, whereas **if you're working in rounds** you'll work in a continual spiral so you won't need to turn the work.

At the end of each row or round, the pattern will give the number of stitches you should have completed in parentheses, so you can confirm that you are doing it right.

Most rounds include a **set of repeated instructions**. This is indicated with symbols which vary from pattern to pattern. This may be brackets () [ ] or asterisks * * around the stitches that are to be repeated. After whichever symbol is chosen will be the number of times these stitches are to be done. For example:

*(sc2tog, sc in the next st) 3 times, 2 sc in the next st.*

Which means you should sc2tog, sc, sc2tog, sc, sc2tog, sc 2 sc. (Check

Glossary for abbreviations).

So an example of a full line of instructions could be:

**Rnd 5: (2 sc in the next st, sc in the next 3 st)6 times (30 st)**

Which may look intimidating to start with, but once you break it all down it much easier to understand.

*Rnd 5:* This is the fifth round in the pattern.

*2 sc in the next st.* Make 2 single crochet stitches, both in the same stitch.

*Sc in the next 3 st.* Make 2 single crochet stitch into each of the next 3 stitches.

*6 times.* Repeat everything inside the brackets 6 times.

*(30 stitches)* You will make a total of 30 stitches in this round.

So as you can see, it's all about breaking down the instructions into workable directions.

# Crochet Terminology

In the list below is some of the crochet terminology which you might come across in patterns. Understanding what it means will make your reading of a pattern more fluent.

*Acrylic* – Synthetic yarn

*Back Loops* - The loops on the top of your crocheting work are the front loops. The ones behind these are the back loops.

*Back Loops Only* - This means to focus only on the back loops.

*Back Loop Single Crochet* - A variation of the single crochet stitch which focuses only on the back loops.

*Coned Yarn* - Yarn that has been wound onto a cone shaped holder.

*Color Flashing* - This is an effect that can happen when using variegated yarn. It's when an unintentional pattern occurs i.e. zig zags.

*Double Crochet* - This stitch is taller than a single crochet stitch and it's formed by the 'Yarn Over' technique.

*Floats* - This describes the unused strands of yarn that are carried across the back of the project.

*Freeform Crochet* - This allows the crocheter explore the craft in unique and unexpected ways.

*Frog* - 'To frog' = to rip out stitches. 'Frogging' = adding functional or decorative pieces, such as buttons.

*Granny Square* - This is a crocheted motif that is made from a ring of chain stitches that is built outwards.

*Half Double Crochet* - These are half a double crochet stitch.

*Inelastic* - This is yarn that is slow to recover its shape (or doesn't at all) once it has been stretched.

*Kitchen Cotton* - This is a yarn that is useful for making projects for kitchen use; potholders, dishcloths, placemats, etc.

***Loops*** - Loops are the integral part of crocheting and are created using the hook.

***PJoining*** - This is using the slip stitch to create beautiful fabrics.

***Place Maker*** - Make a mark on your work (preferably one that can easily be removed) to help you locate a spot later.

***Plarn*** - 'Plastic Yarn'- often plastic bags that have been cut up and repurposed into yarn.

***Protein Fiber*** - A fiber made from protein.

***Scrapghan*** - An afghan created from yarn scraps.

***Shell Stitch*** - Works multiple stitches into one single stitch.

***Self-Striping Yarn*** - A type of variegated yarn which has two or more colors. Often there are long lengths of each color before it changes.

***Single Crochet*** - A basic crochet stitch.

***Slipstitch*** - A loose stitch joining layers of fabric which isn't visible externally.

***Tapestry Needle*** - A hand sewing needle that's useful for adding embroidery.

***Turning Chain*** - A group of stitches that facilitates the transition between the rows of crochet stitches.

***Treble Crochet*** - A taller stitch than the double crochet.

***Variegated Yarn*** - Yarn that has variety throughout.

***Work Even*** - Continuing in the same stitch patter, without increasing or decreasing.

***Worsted Weight Yarn*** - A medium weight yarn.

***Yarn Cake*** - A method for winding yarn.

***Yarn Over*** - This is a stitch which involves wrapping the yarn from back to front before placing the hook in the stitch.

# CROCHET PATTERN BASICS

## Starting A Crochet Pattern

When beginning a crochet project, **the first thing you'll want to do is create a slip knot on your hook** – which is never stated in the pattern, but is assumed.

**To create your slip knot, simply follow the steps below:**

1. Put the short piece on top of the long yarn.

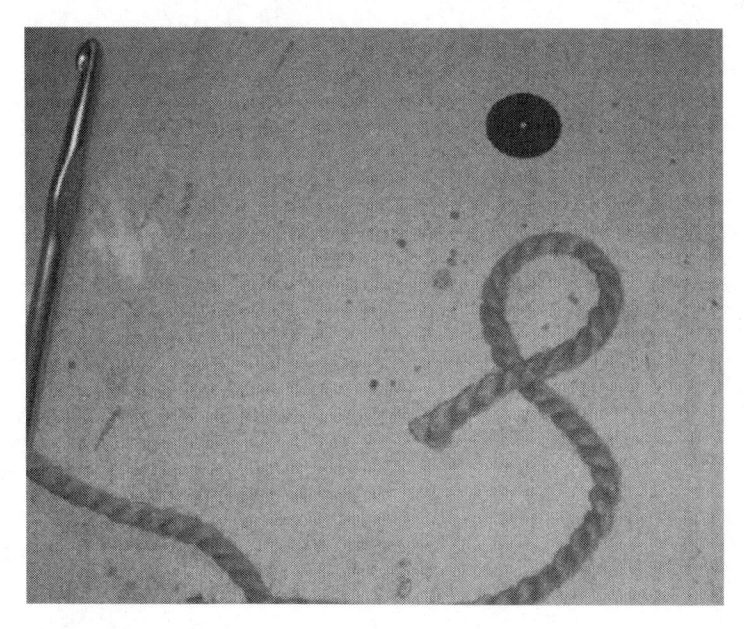

2. Next, flip down the whole thing onto the longer yarn. This is a test to see if this is going to go over to the next line properly

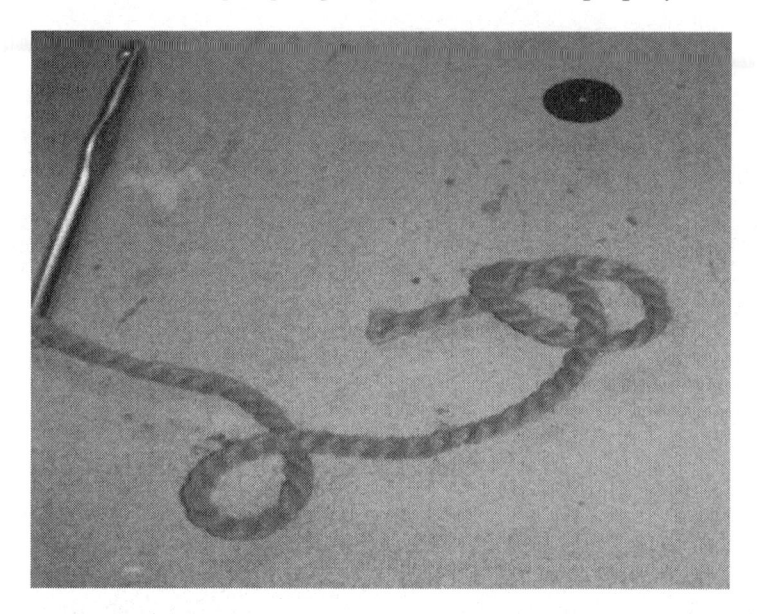

3. Hold the middle yarn between your thumb & forefinger.

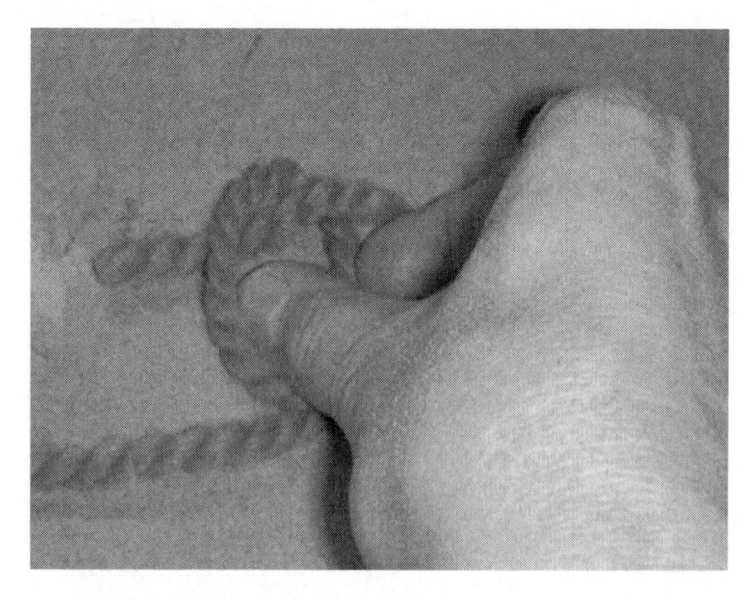

4. Pull out the middle yarn gently.

CROCHET AFGHANS

5. Hang on to tail and pull the loop tight.

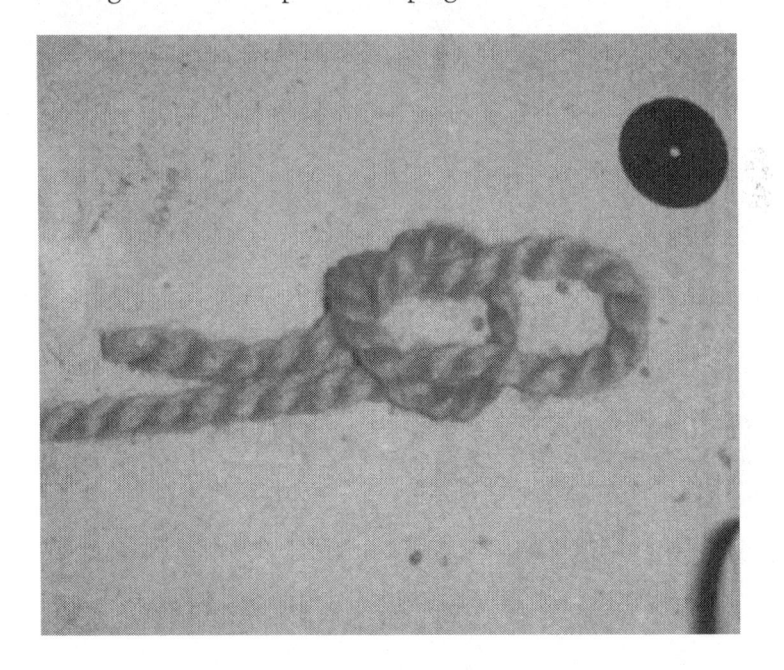

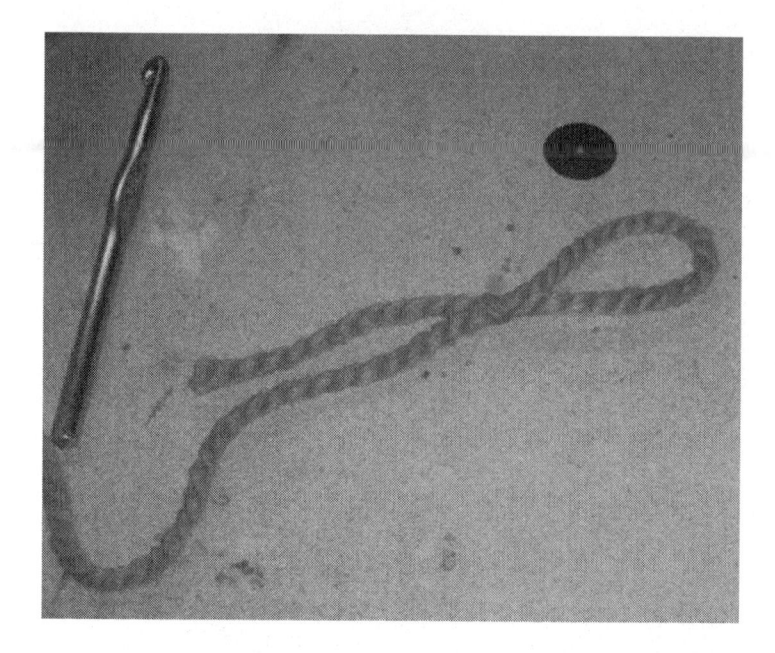

Once you have done this, you'll want to **create the Foundation Chain** at the length specified in the pattern. This may be written in one of two ways:

*Row 1: Ch 20, sc in 2nd ch from hook and in each ch across.*

*Ch 20.*

*Row 1: Sc in 2nd ch from hook and in each ch across.*

These mean exactly the same thing: make a chain of 20 stitches loosely. A chain stitch is created by holding the end of the slip knot between your thumb and middle finger, then wrapping the yarn from back to front around the shaft of your hook. You will then use the hook to draw the yarn through the loop on the hook, as demonstrated by the step-by-step guide below:

**Steps 1 & 2:** Begin the chain by picking up the loop in your left hand.

CROCHET AFGHANS

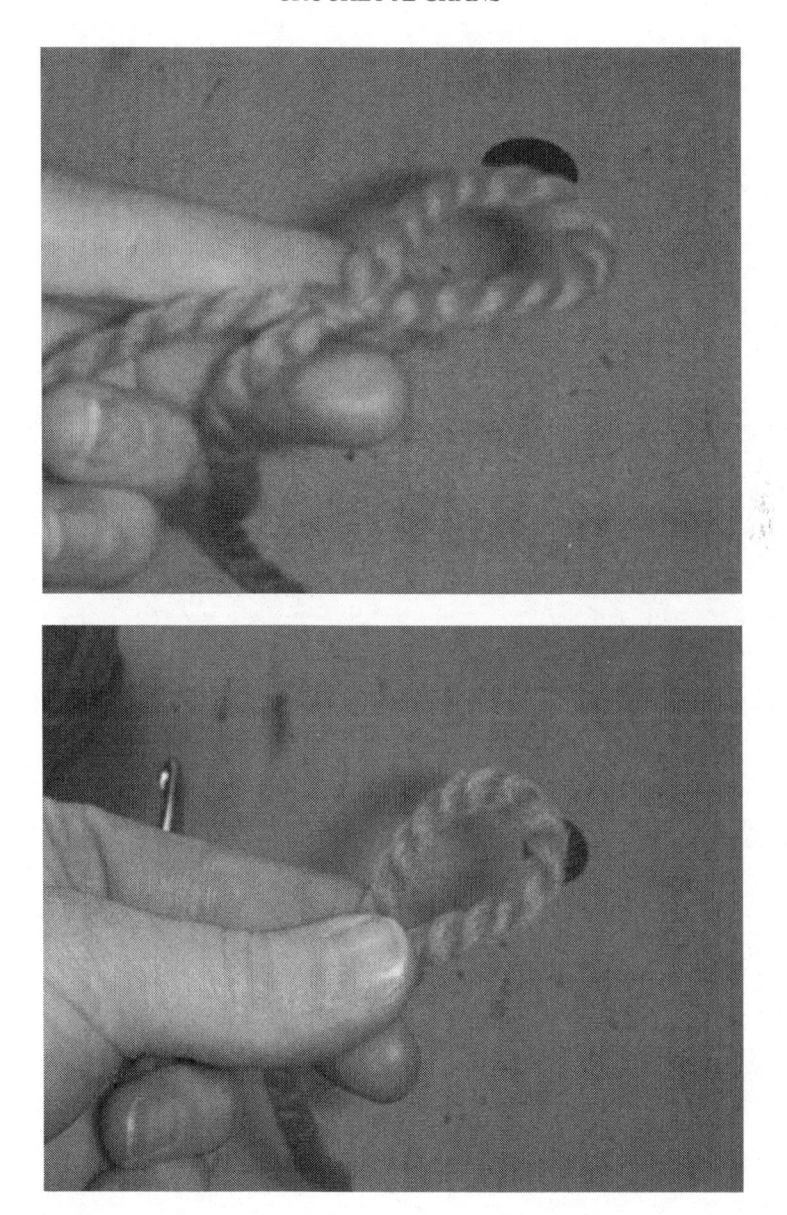

**Steps 3 & 4:** Slip the hook into the ring and make tighter the ring around the hook.

**Step 5:** In the 2nd chain from the hook insert the head of the crochet hook.

CROCHET AFGHANS

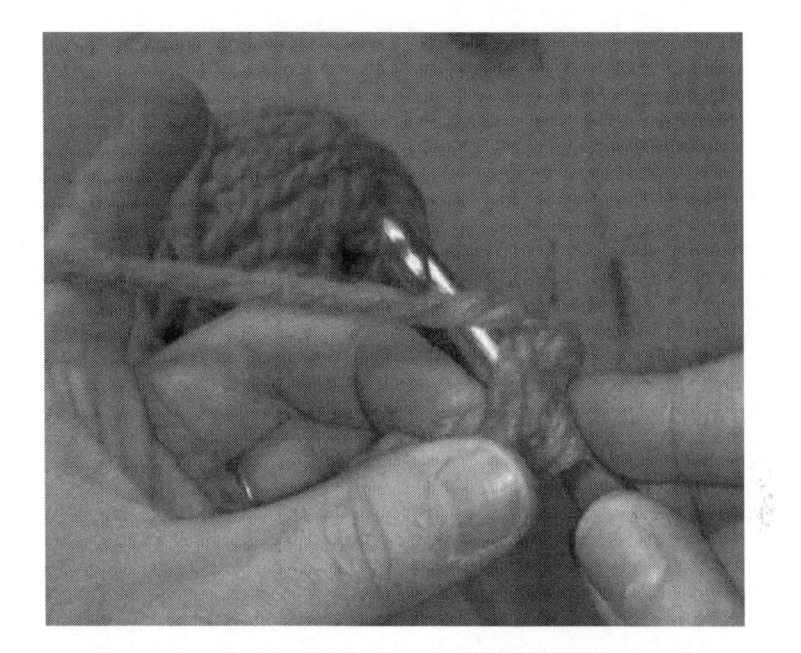

**Step 6:** Catch the yarn now in your left hand with the hook.

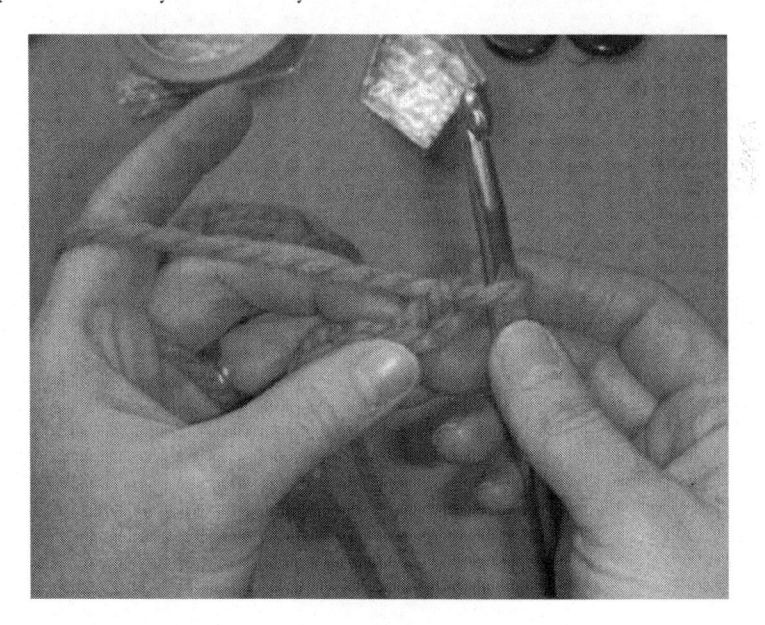

**Step 7:** Pull it through both loops of the stitch.

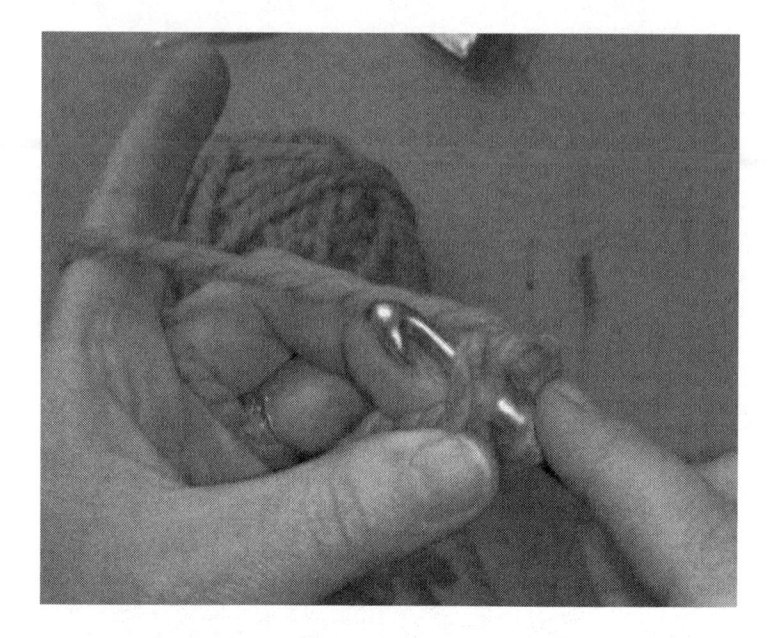

**Step 8:** This will leave you with 2 loops on your hook.

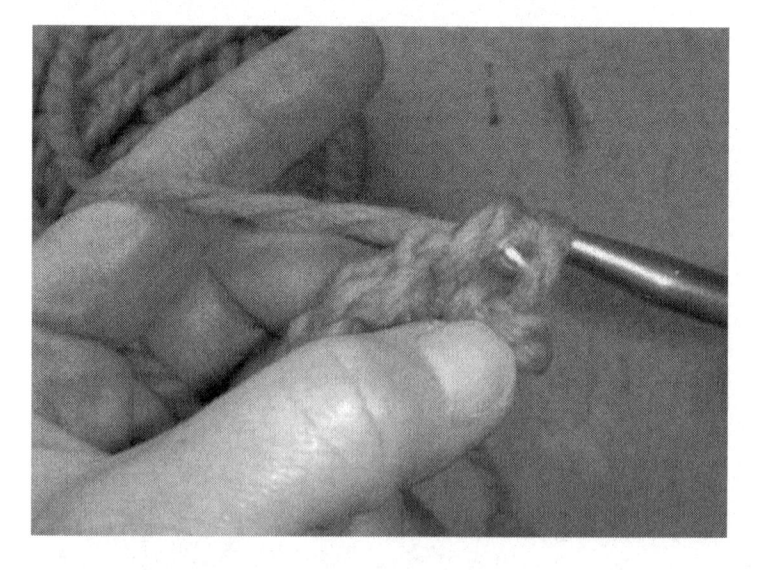

**Step 9:** Catch the yarn in your left hand with the hook again.

CROCHET AFGHANS

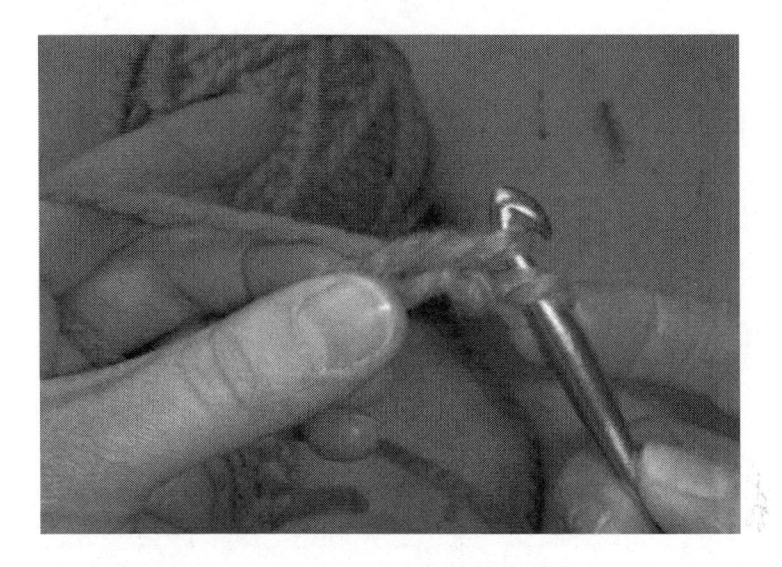

**Steps 10 & 11:** Pull it through both loops on the hook.

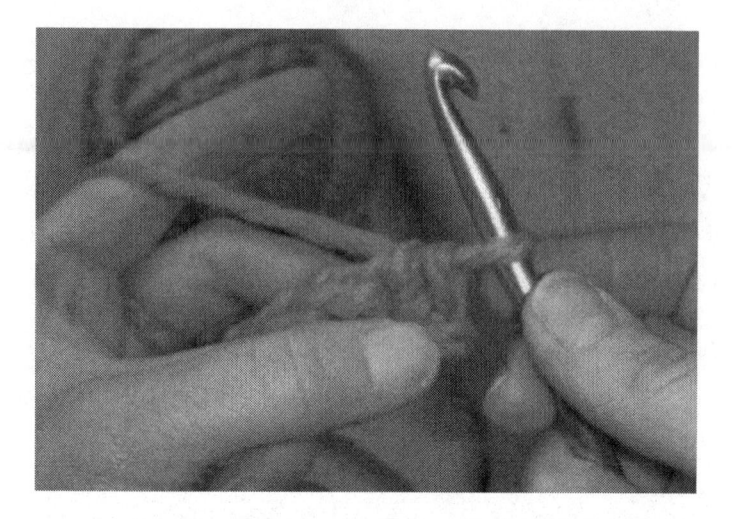

**Step 12:** Repeat these Steps until you get to the end of the chained row.

Once you have completed your foundation chain, be sure to **count the stitches carefully**, but be sure **not to include the slip knot** in that – the loop on the hook is never counted as a stitch.

When you have done this, you will complete the second part of the instruction '*sc in 2nd ch from hook*' which means that you'll start crocheting from the second chain (or stitch) away from the hook.

Now that you have completed the first row, it is time to turn your work (if you're working in rows) and move onto the next set of instructions.

# Finishing Project

To finish off you crochet project, you'll want to fasten the yarn:

- Cut the yarn about 6 inches away from the hook.

- Using the hook, draw the cut end of the yarn through the last remaining loop on your hook.

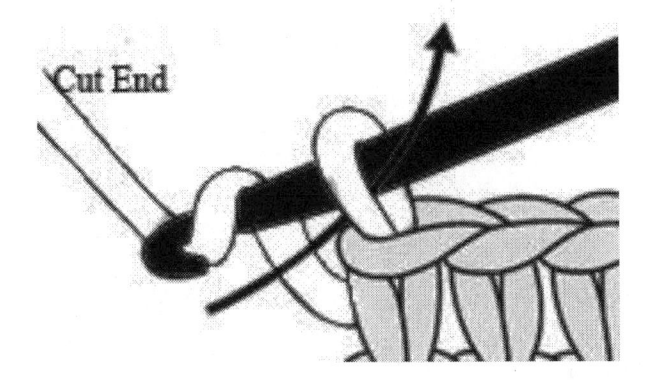

- Pull gently on the yarn to finish off the work.

- Thread the remaining yarn tail onto a yarn needle.

- Weave the 6 inch tail of yarn up and down through 3 or 4 stitches in a zig zag pattern.

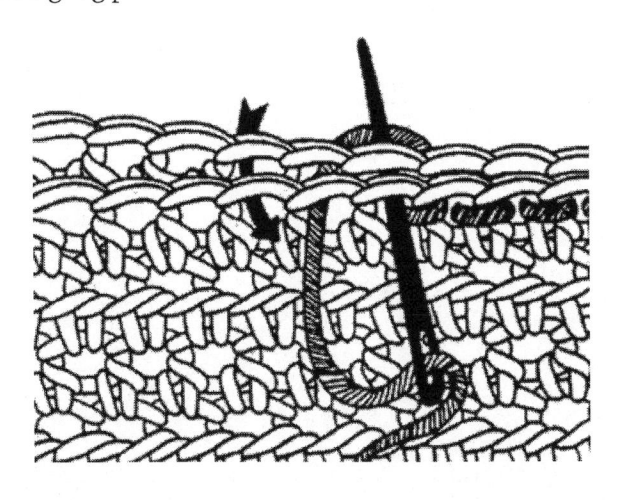

- Do the same going back the way you came.

- Cut the yarn about ¼ inch from the fabric and gently pull the fabric which will make the end disappear whilst keeping your work secure.

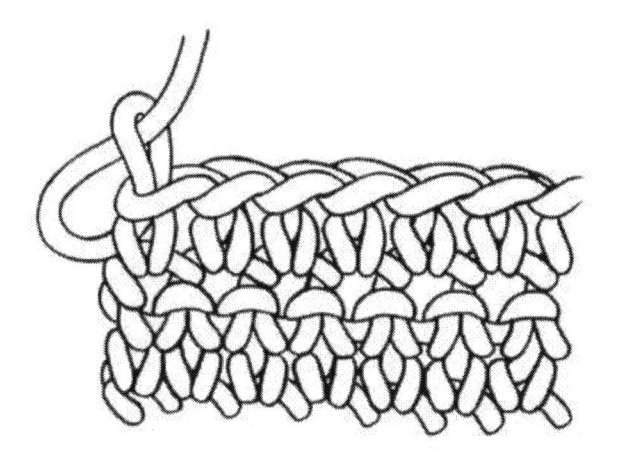

# BASIC STITCHES

There are a few stitches that you will need to get to grips with to crochet your afghan. **Step-by-step guides for these stitches** are included in this chapter.

## Single Crochet Stitch

If the instruction tells you to create a single crochet stitch – or **SC** – you will want to do this:

1. Make your Slip Knot

2. Bring your yarn over the hook from back to front and grab it with the hook.

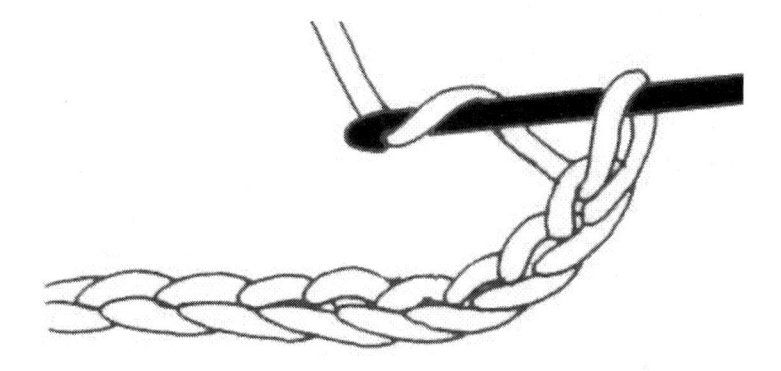

3. Draw the hooked yarn through the slip knot and onto the hook.

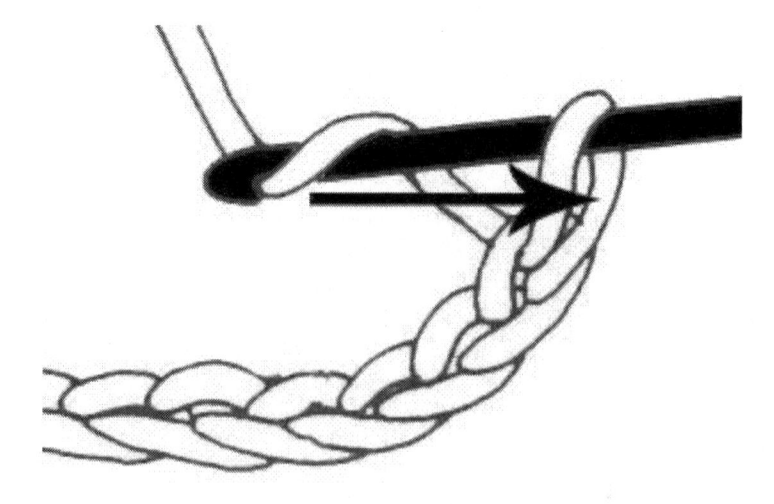

4. Skip the first chain stitch.

CROCHET AFGHANS

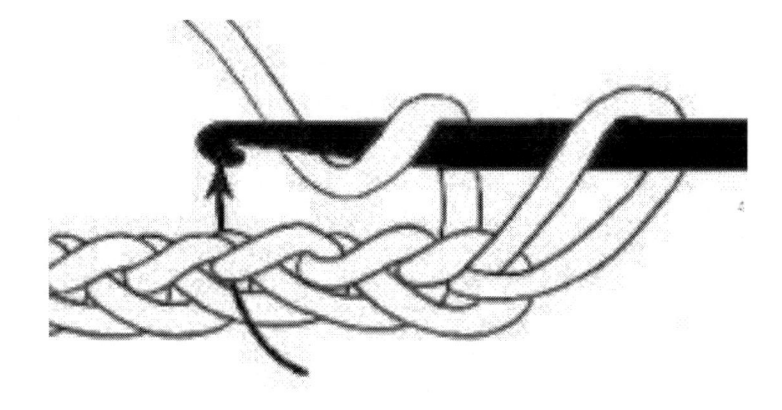

5. Insert the hook into the center of the next chain stitch and draw the yarn through the stitch and up onto the hook. You will now have two loops.

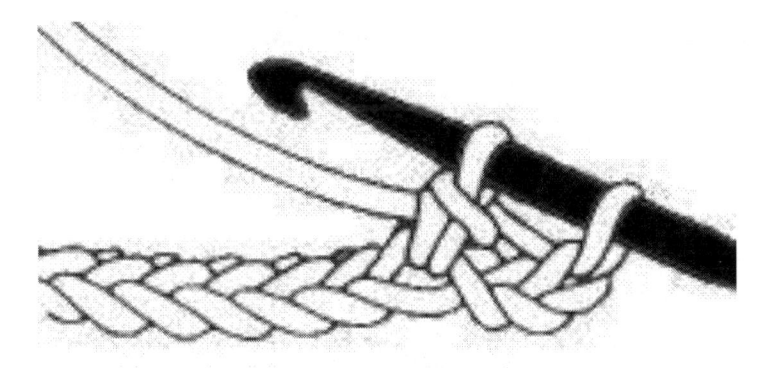

6. Bring the yarn over the hook from back to front and draw it through both loops on the hook. One loop remains on the hook – this is your single crochet stitch.

## Double Crochet Stitch

If your pattern wants you to create a double crochet stitch – or **DC** – you'll do the following:

1. Make your Slip Knot stitch and create your foundation chain.

2. Bring your yarn over the hook from back to front and grab it with the hook.

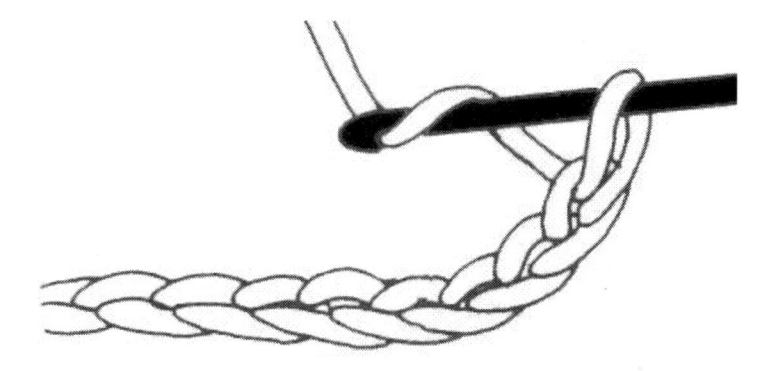

3. Insert the hook into the fourth chain from the hook.

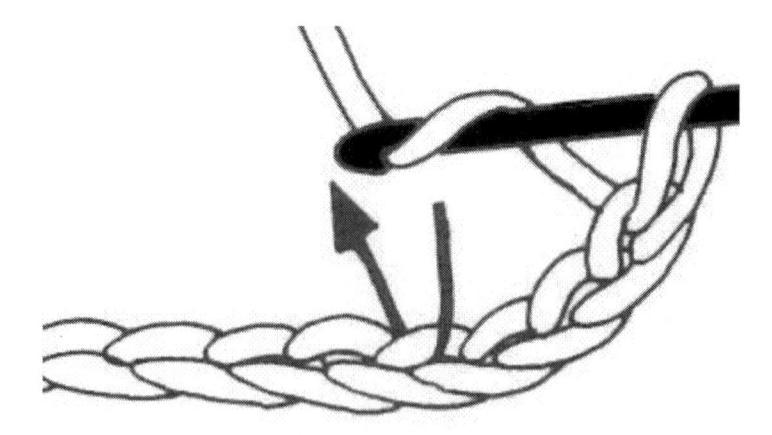

4. Draw the yarn over the hook and pull it through the chain. You should now have three loops on the hook.

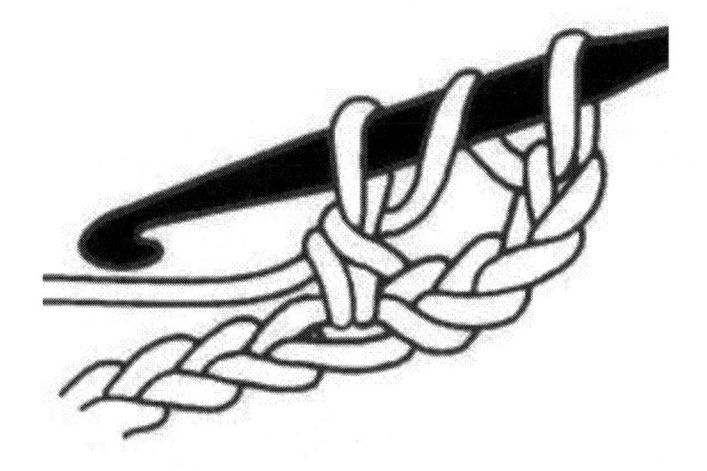

5. Yarn over and pull through two loops on the hook.

6. Yarn over again and pull through the remaining two loops – a double crochet stitch has been made.

# Afghan Stitch

To create an afghan stitch, which is shaped like little squares with two horizontal strands and a vertical bar on top of them, you will need a special hook. **Afghan hooks** are longer and available in a variety of shapes and sizes.

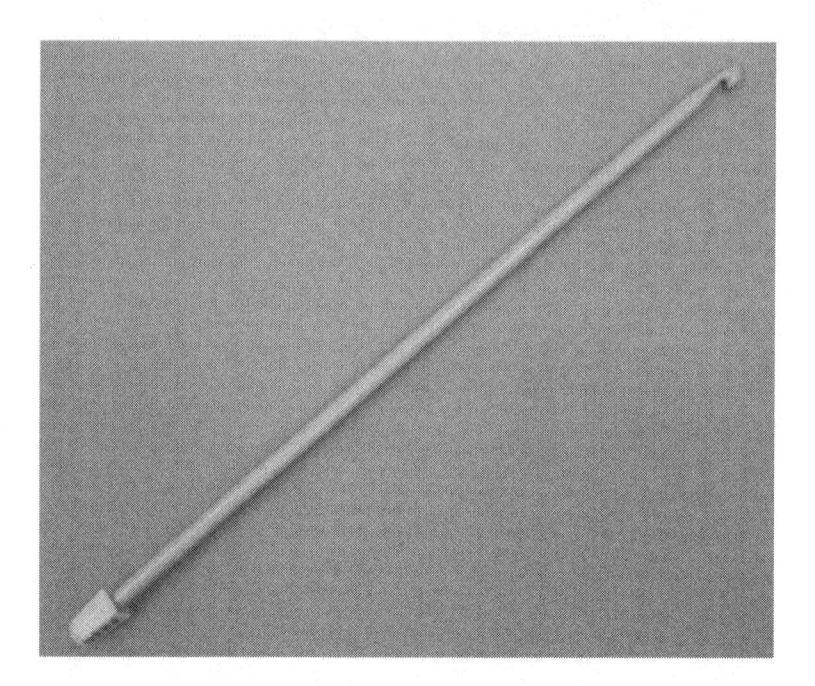

***To create an afghan stitch, you need to:***

1. Chain 16 stitches as a foundation chain.

2. Insert your hook in the second chain from the hook.

3. Yarn over the hook and draw your yarn through the chain stitch.

CROCHET AFGHANS

4. Insert your hook into the next chain and repeat the proceeding step in each chain across the foundation chain.

5. Yarn over hook and draw the yarn through one loop on the hook.

6. Yarn over hook and draw the yarn through the next two loops on the hook.

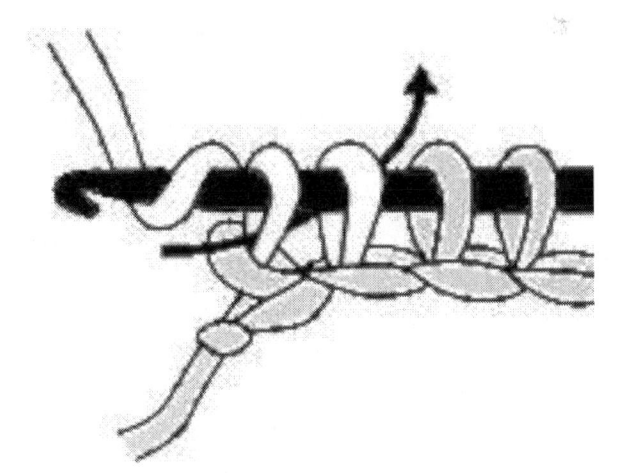

7. Insert your hook behind the next vertical bar in the row below.

8. Yarn over the hook and draw the yarn through the stitch.

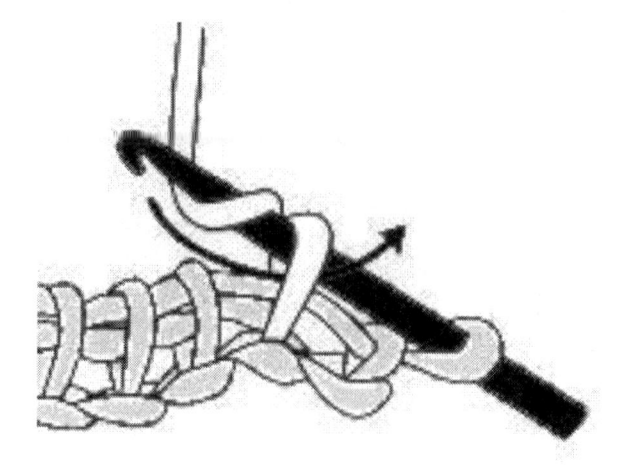

9. Insert your hook under the last two vertical bars at the end of the row.

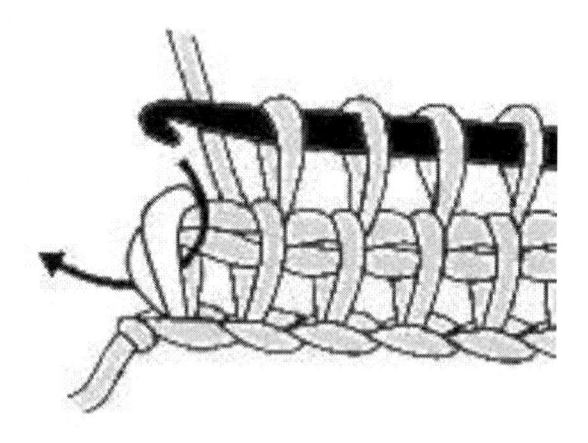

10. Yarn over hook and draw your yarn through both vertical bars.

11. Yarn over hook and draw the yarn through one loop on the hook.

12. Yarn over hook and draw the yarn through the next two loops on the hook.

13. Continue working until you are complete.

14. Work a slip stitch under each vertical bar across the last row to finish the swatch.

# Slip Stitch

Slip stitches are a way to create 'invisible' stitches. If your afghan crochet pattern requires you to do one, you will want to:

- Insert the hook front to back under the top of the second chain from the hook.

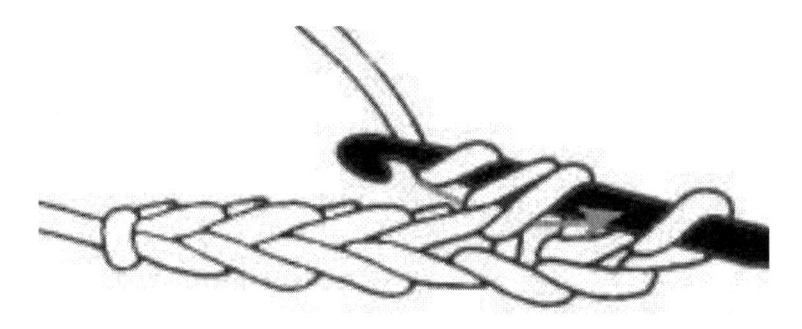

- Yarn over the hook, then pull the yarn through both loops on the hook, leaving you with just one loop.

# Chain Stitch and Turning Chains

A chain stitch is a series of looped stitches to form a chain like pattern, which as you have seen, is crucial to crocheting. How chain stitches are created, is described in the 'Starting a Crochet Pattern' section of this guide earlier in this chapter. You will want to crochet a turning chain – or *t-ch* – after you have completed a chain and turned your work, to ensure your work is all in line. This stitch is not counted in the rest of the chain.

The number of stitches you will want in your turning chain, depends on what you are working with. Below is a list demonstrating this:

| Working Stitches | Turning Chains Needed |
| --- | --- |
| Slip Stitch | 0 |
| Single Crochet | 1 |
| Half Double Crochet | 2 |
| Double Crochet | 3 |
| Triple Crochet | 4 |

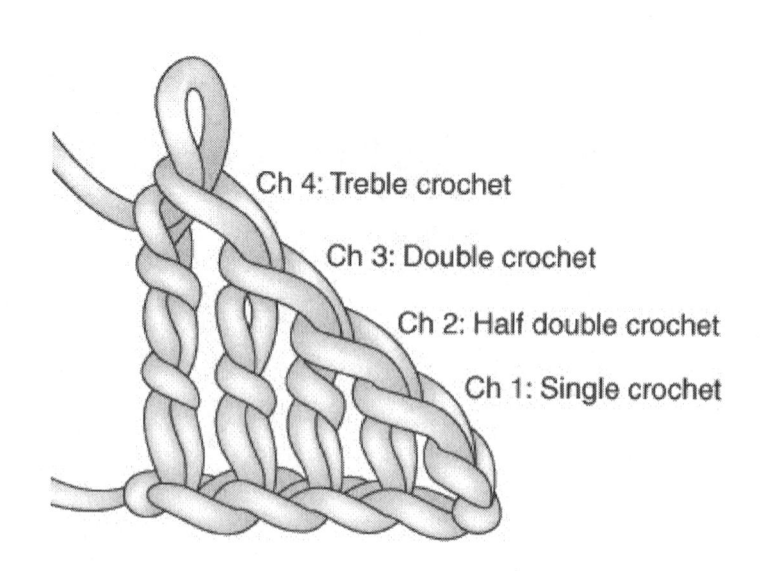

Ch 4: Treble crochet

Ch 3: Double crochet

Ch 2: Half double crochet

Ch 1: Single crochet

# TECHNIQUES

There are crocheting techniques that help creating an afghan a much easier process. To help you with these, they will be included in this chapter.

## Yarn over Hook

Wrapping the yarn over your crochet hook is called Yarn Over – or *Yo* – and it's the most basic step to every crochet stitch. That being said, it must be done right or you won't be able to draw the yarn smoothly onto the next stitch. To do this, you need to:

1. Slide your slip knot to the shaft of your hook.

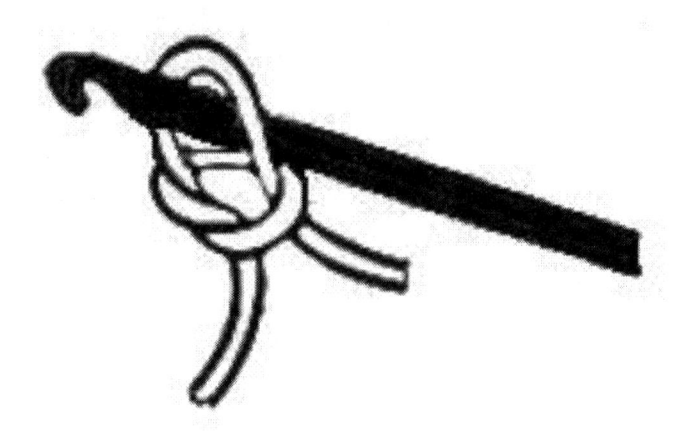

2. With your yarn hand, hold the tail of the slip knot between your thumb and middle finger.

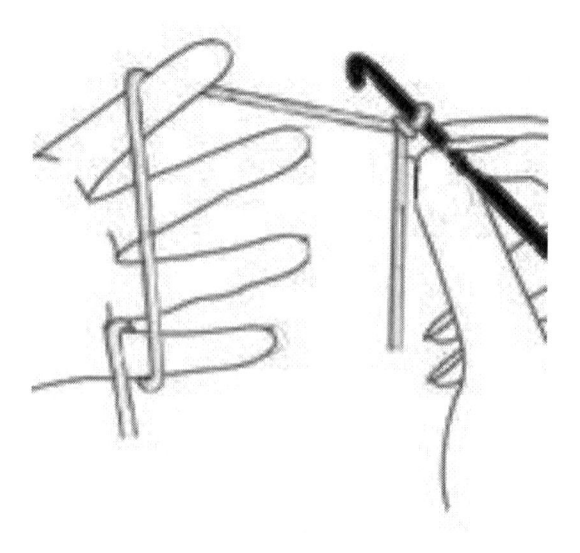

3. Using the forefinger on your yarn hand, bring the yarn up behind the hook.

4. Lay the yarn over the shaft, positioned between the slip knot and the throat of the hook.

## Increases and Decreases

**To increase** – or *inc* – in crochet, you simply work in more than stitch, as specified by the pattern, into the same hole. This will increase the number of stitches in the current row you're working on in comparison to the previous row.

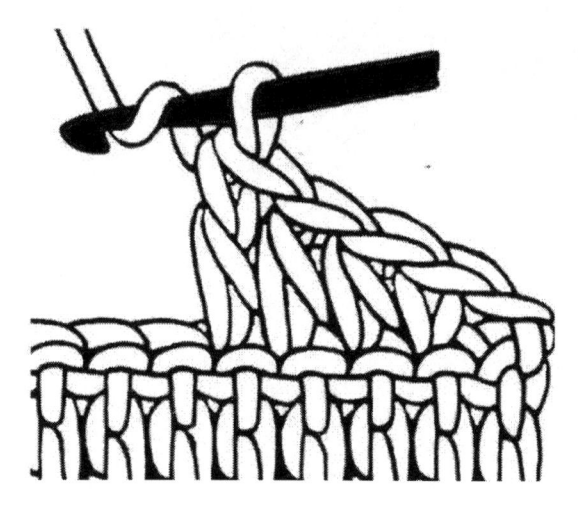

**To decrease** – or *dec* – you work in the first stitch as specified, skipping the final step of the stitch. This is the part where you draw a final loop through the loops on your hook, which leaves the worked loops on the crochet hook, before moving onto the next stitch. When you have completed the second stitch, you'll draw the yarn through all of the stitches on your hook, to draw the first and second stitch together, leaving you with less stitches in the current row in comparison to the previous row.

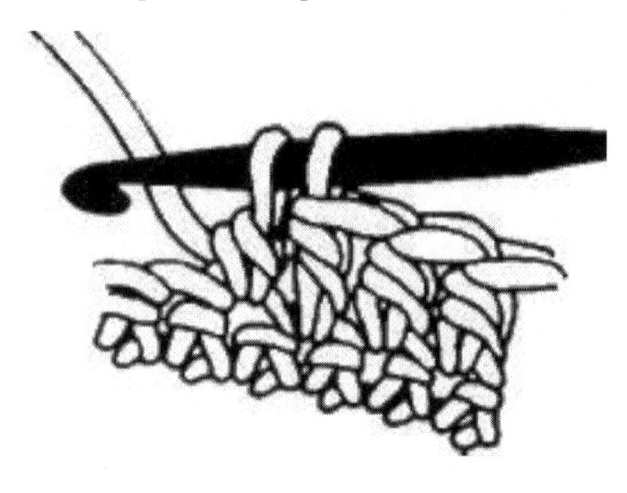

# Changing Colors

Once you have started crocheting, there will be a point in which you'll want to change the color of the yarn you're using. To do this, you need to:

1. Start the work in color A.

2. When you're at the point that you wish to change, work as far as the last single stitch in the row or round, but leave the final stitch unfinished.

3. Grab color B with your crochet hook.

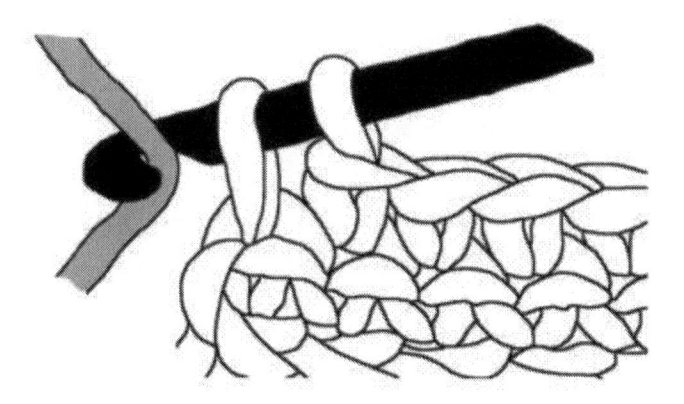

4. Pull up a loop with color B. You may need to gently tug the yarn of color A to keep the loops from getting too big.

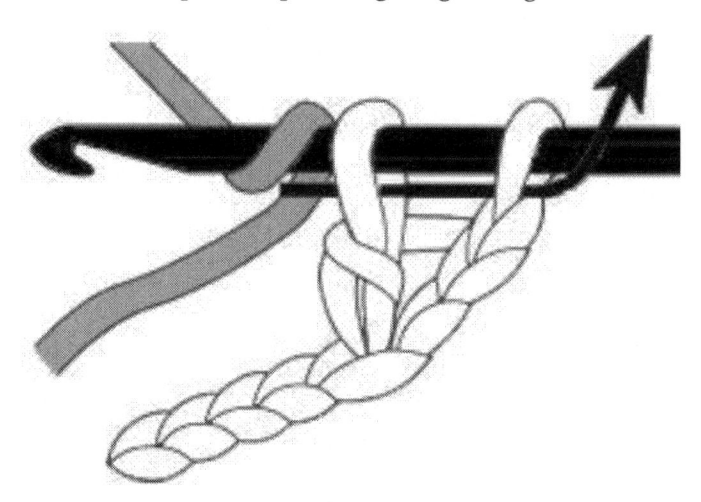

5. You then need to decide whether or not to cut color A. If you're going to use it again within the next few rows, it is better left as it is, but if not then you'll want to cut the yarn with approximately six inches to spare, which you'll weave in later.

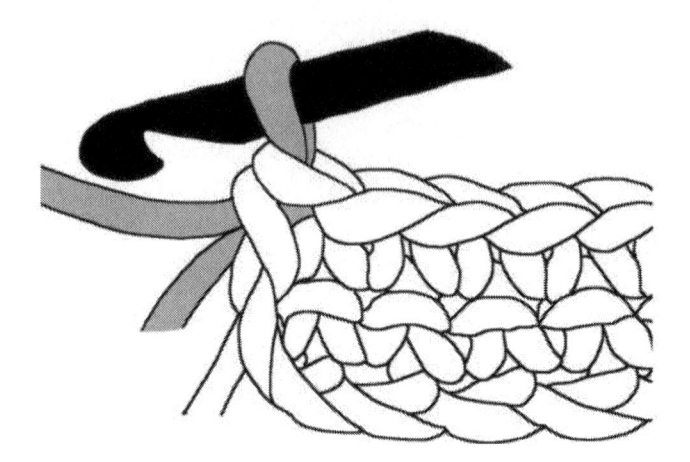

CROCHET AFGHANS

# Working in the Round

Some afghan patterns will require you to work in rounds. To do this, you first need to create the center ring and crochet the first round. After you complete the number of stitches needed in the first round, join the first and last stitches to complete the circle. Here are the steps to do this:

1. Chain 6 stitches then insert your hook into the first chain stitch you made, forming a ring.

2. Draw the yarn over your hook, then pull it through the stitch and loop it onto your hook, completing your center ring.

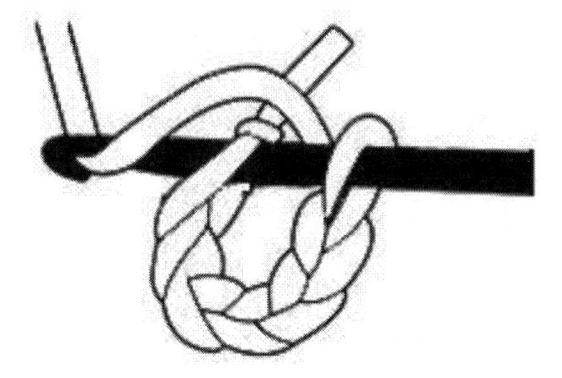

3. Chain 1 stitch, making the turning chain for a single crochet.

4. Insert your hook into the center ring.

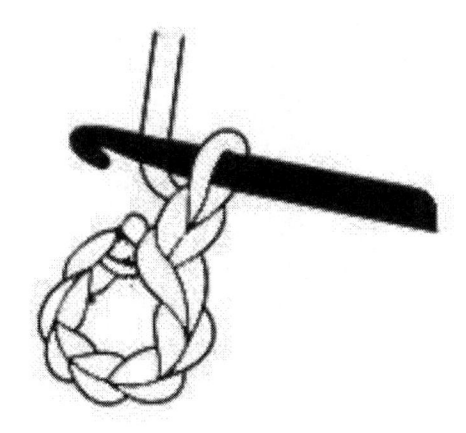

5. Yarn over your hook and draw the yarn through the center ring.

6. Yarn over your hook and draw the yarn through the 2 loops on your hook.

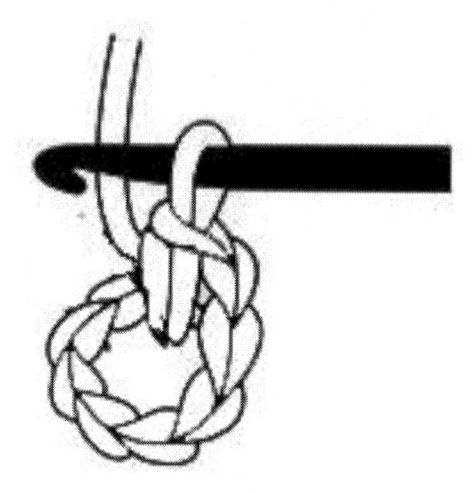

7. Continue to work single crochet stitches into the ring until you cannot fit anymore.

8. Insert your hook under the 2 top loops of the first single crochet stitch you made.

9. Yarn over your hook and draw the yarn through the stitch and the loop on your hook to complete a slip stitch.

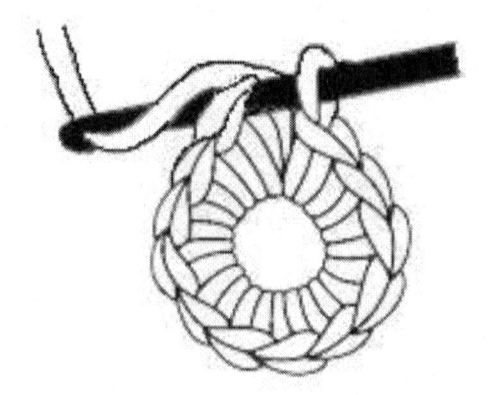

10. Chain 3 stitches to create the turning chain.

11. Work 1 double crochet stitch under the top 2 loops of the first stitch, the stitch directly below the turning chain. Remember, you do not need to turn your work.

12. Work 2 double crochet stitches into each stitch around, then join the first and the last stitch of the round with a slip stitch, completing the round.

# Joining Yarn

This is an important step in crocheting, because if you reach the end of a ball of yarn, but need to continue the project, you want this to be seamless to not spoil the appearance of your work. To do this, follow these steps:

1. Double crochet across the row, stopping before the last stitch of the row.

2. Work the last double crochet stitch to the point where 2 loops are left on the hook.

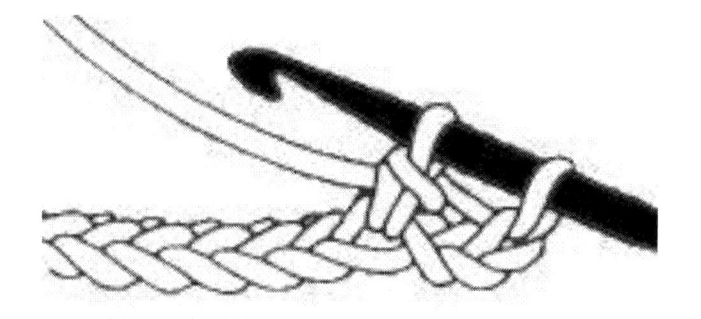

3. Wrap the end of the new yarn around the hook, from back to front.

4. Draw the new yarn through the 2 loops on your hook.

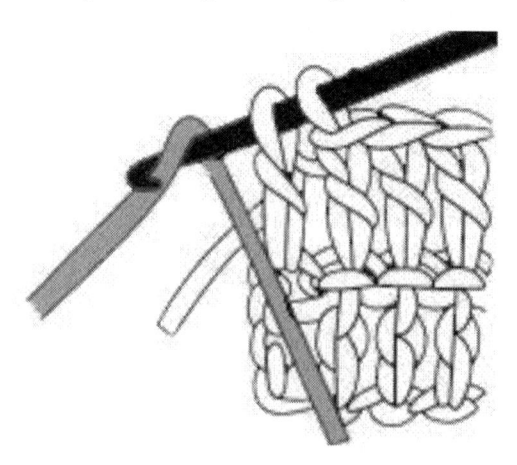

5. Tug on the dropped end of the old yarn at the base of the double crochet to tighten up the stitch.

6. Remove the loop from your hook.

7. Insert your hook into the top of the last double crochet down through the center of the stitch.

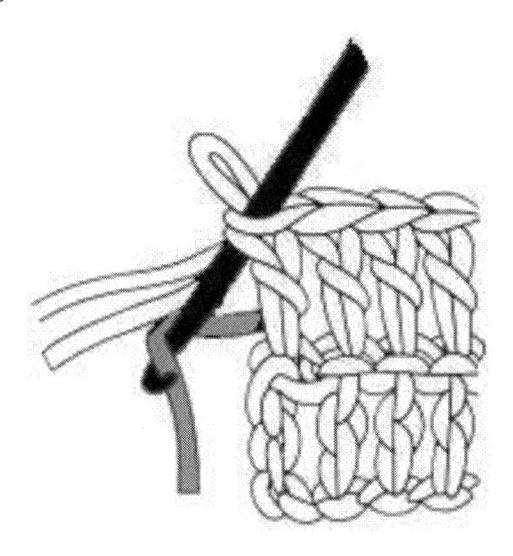

8. Yarn over using the end of the old yarn at the bottom of the stitch.

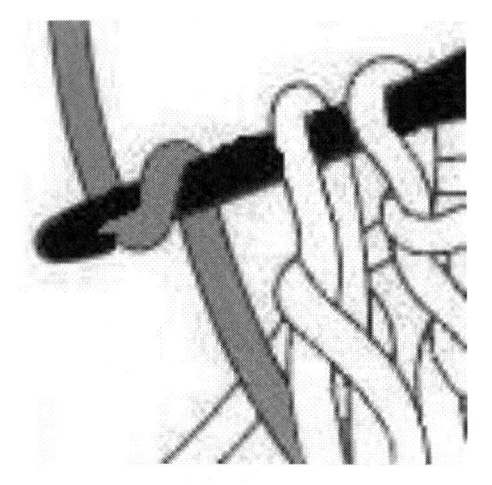

9. Draw the tail end up through the stitch.

10. Stick your hook back through the hoop to begin your next row.

## Sewing Together

If you are creating your afghan using squares, you will need to stitch these together. A great way to join crocheted pieces together is by using a technique called the whip stitch.

1. Align the pieces you'd like to join together.

2. Weave the yarn back and forth through several stitches on one of the pieces to secure the end. Remember to match the yarn to the pieces you're joining for a better effect.

3. Insert the needle and pull the yarn through the inside loops of the first 2 corresponding stitches of the pieces to be joined. Pull the yarn tight enough to join the pieces, but not too tight, distorting the pieces.

4. Draw the yarn up and over the 2 loops of the first stitch.

5. Repeat the last step through the entire edges to be joined.

6. At the end of the seam, weave the yarn back and forth through several stitches to secure.

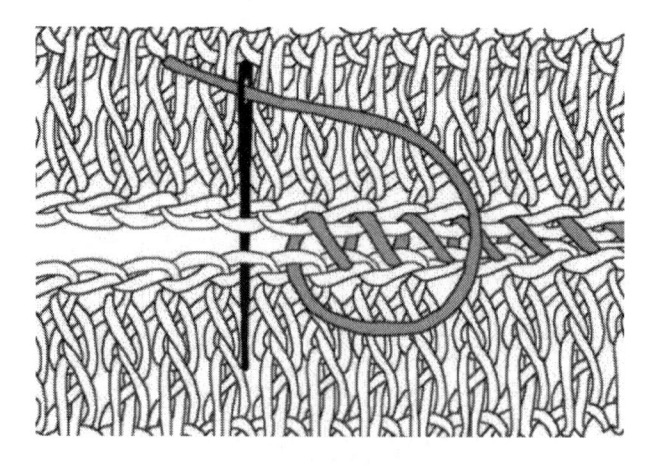

# ADVANCED STITCHES

When you have practiced crocheting, you may want to add some extra features to your afghan to make it more special to you. This chapter includes some wonderful stitches you might like to try.

# Ridges

Ridges can be crocheted for a number of reasons; to add detail to a design, to finish something off nicely or even to give a textured effect. To do this, you need to:

1. Make your Slip Knot stitch and create your foundation chain.

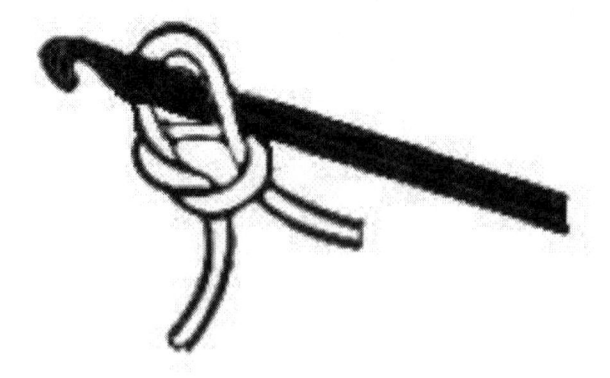

2. Start with a double crochet stitch and repeat this along the row.

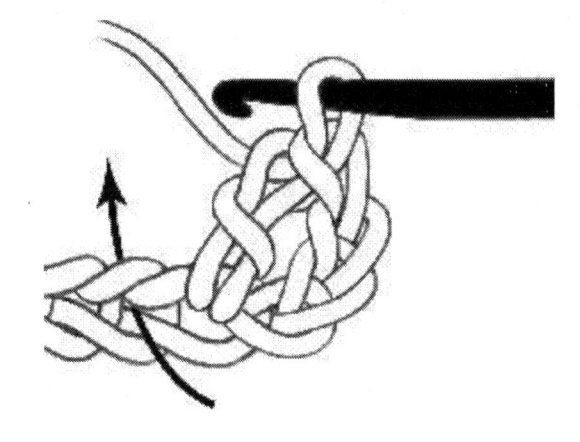

3. Don't turn your work; instead work in single crochet stitches from left to right.

4. Create a slip stitch in the turn chain to end this row.

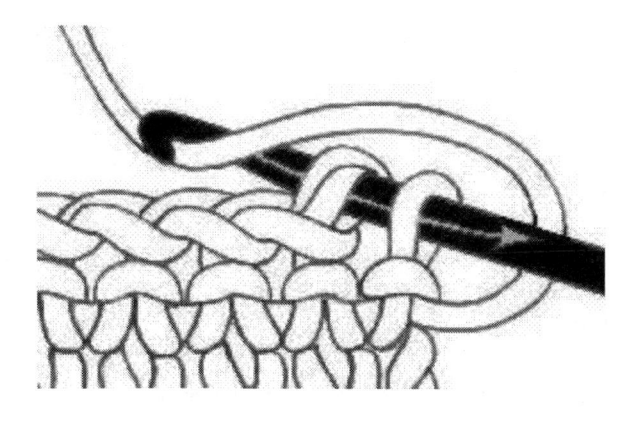

5. Chain 3 stitches and skip the first stitch to create a double crochet stitch in the back loop of the second stitch away from the hook.

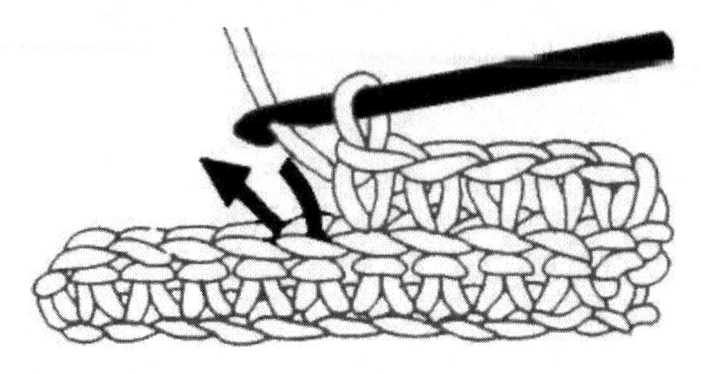

6. Repeat these steps until you have the ridge that you desire.

# Shell Borders

Shell borders are very popular as they give a crochet afghan a pretty edge, without being too fussy or difficult to do. To crochet a shell stitch:

1. Make a slip knot and crochet your foundation chain.

2. Work in a single crochet stitch into the second chain from your hook.

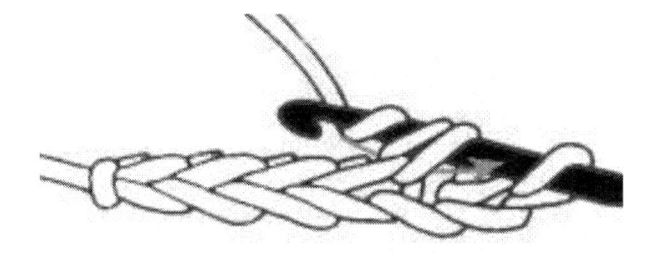

3. Skip the next two chain stitches, then work in a double crochet stitch into the next chain after that.

4. Work four more double crochet stitches into the same chain stitch, completing five double chain stitches.

5. Skip the next two chain stitches, then work a single crochet stitch in the next chain after that.

6. Skip the next two chain stitches and start over again.

# Picots

The picot stitch is usually used as edging and added onto a finished afghan. You can either start along the edge of something you have already created, or begin by creating a foundation chain of stitches.

1. Single crochet in the first stitch, then chain 3 stitches and single crochet in the next stitch.

2. Single crochet in the next 3 stitches.

3. Chain 3 and single crochet in the next stitch – forming the picot.

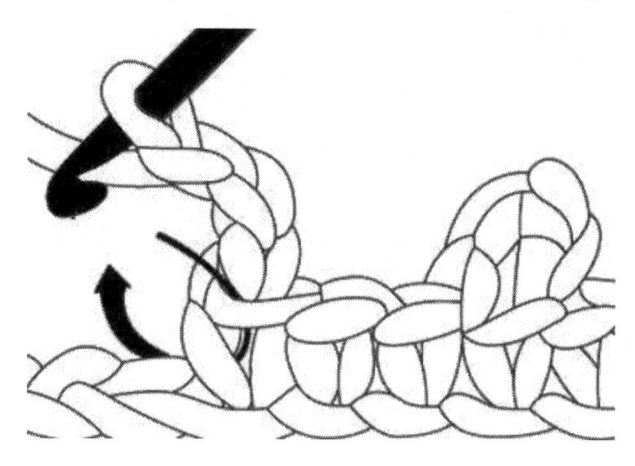

4. Repeat steps 2 and 3 until you reach the end of your work to create

a chain.

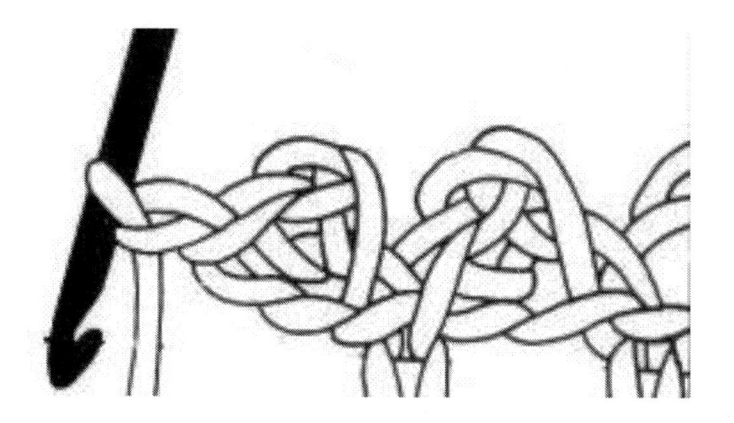

# Reverse Stitch

The reverse stitch is sometimes referred to as a crab stitch which creates a twisted, rounded edge that's great for finishing off a project. It's done like this:

1. Insert your crochet hook from front to back, in the next stitch to the right. Be sure to have the right side of your work facing you.

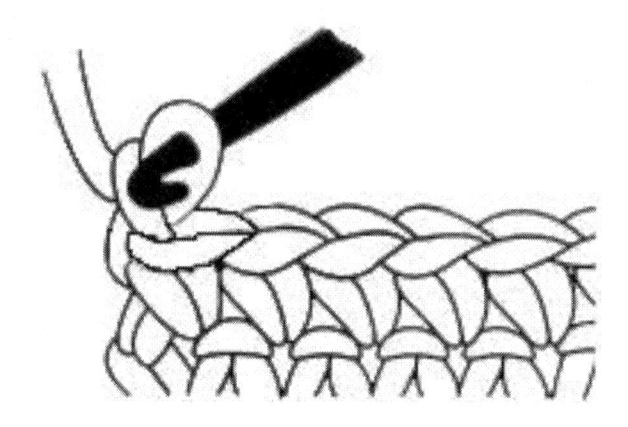

2. Yarn over and draw the yarn through the stitch in a similar way to how you do a single crochet stitch – just in reverse.

3. Yarn over and draw the yarn through the 2 loops on your hook completing one single reverse crochet stitch.

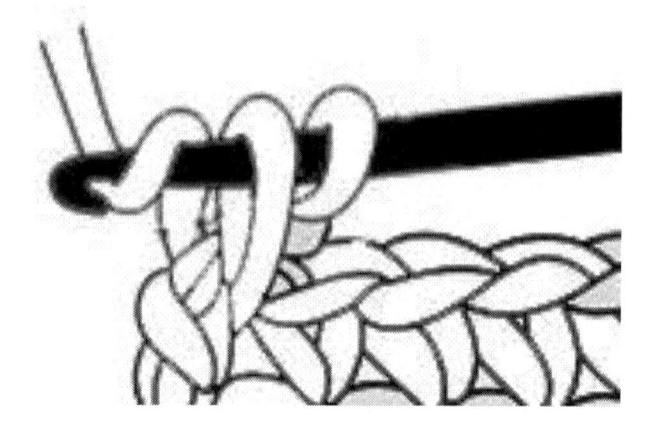

## Cluster Stitch

The cluster stitch is made up of a number of stitches that are half closed, then joined together as described below.

1. Make a slip knot and create your foundation chain.

2. Yarn over hook, insert hook into the next stitch.

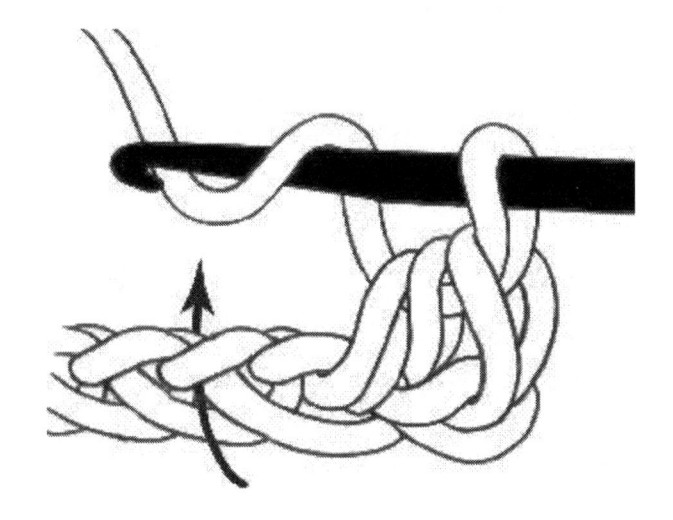

3. Yarn over, draw yarn through the stitch.

4. Yarn over, draw through 2 loops on the hook.

5. Repeat steps 2 to 4 three times.

6. Yarn over and draw through the 5 loops on the hook. This completes a cluster created with 4 double crochet stitches.

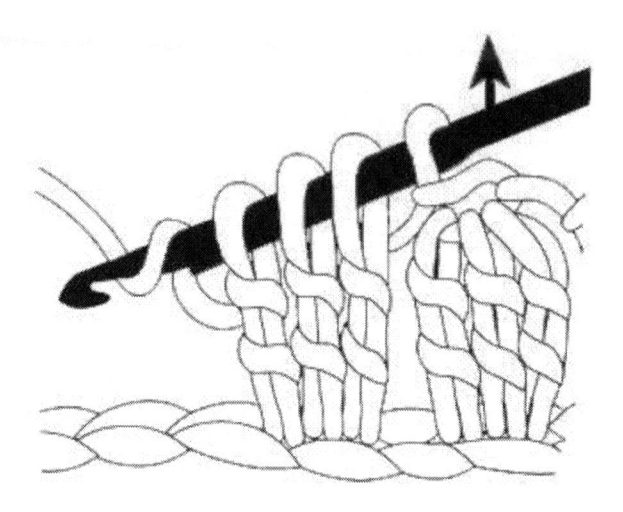

# CROCHETING TIPS

Before taking a look at some patterns, there is a few things that you might wish to consider when crocheting an afghan. These will be looked at in this chapter.

# Gauge Swatch

It is essential to crochet a gauge swatch – especially when you are just starting out – because it gives you a sense of what the finished fabric will be like. The gauge will ensure that the stitches remain consistent and the size of your finished project will be correct. Patterns generally recommend that you make a swatch, and give you the necessary information for it.

This information will also include the recommended crochet hook and yarn weight. Of course, if you chose to adjust this to your personal requirements, you can use the gauge instructions to check that it will work.

Crocheters often crochet tighter at the beginning and the end of rows, so if the gauge requires 7 stitches to equal 2 inches, be sure to swatch at least a 4 inch square, to make sure the measurements are correct.

## Crocheting Left-Handed

Being left-handed needn't stop you learning to crochet. It may seem challenging at first, after all most patterns are aimed at right-handed users, and attempting to manage these will have you working backwards. Below are a few ways to get around this:

1. Reverse the pattern so that you're holding the crochet hook in your right hand. This means that the 'wrong side' of the pattern is actually 'the right side'.

2. Practice holding the hook until you're comfortable. A lot of left-handed crocheters have created their own variation on the 'pencil' or 'knife' hold, into a way that suits them.

3. Learn by sitting across from someone right–handed, mirroring their movements!

# Avoid Common Mistakes

It is very common to make mistakes in crochet; even the most experienced crocheter will make small errors from time to time, so the most important thing is not to get disheartened if you do. There are, however, a few things you can be aware of to minimize things going wrong:

- ***Use the right yarn*** – Patterns will very often specify what you will need to make a project successfully. Be sure to take this into account when purchasing the yarn you'll use for your afghan.

- ***Uneven tension*** – Ensuring the tension stays the same will make sure that your end product is the perfect size. Hold your yarn in the right way and take regular breaks to ensure the tension is equal.

- ***Miscounting stitches*** – Patterns will often tell you how many stitches you should have crocheted at the end of each row. Even the most experienced crocheter can make a mistake when counting, so be sure to double check!

- ***Loops*** – Sometimes, crocheters will insert the hook into the wrong loop which affects the entire project. Don't get too tired to prevent yourself from making this error.

- ***Turning chains*** – Never skip a space after the turning chain, which is a very common mistake for beginners. It's easily fixed by unravelling what you have done and starting the row again.

# AFGHAN PATTERNS

Now that you have seen all of the stitches, techniques and tips in this guide, it is time to view and practice some afghan patterns. The following chapter will give you examples of the different kind of afghans you can create, ranging from beginner to advanced.

# BEGINNER

## Baby Blanket

A baby blanket is a fast, easy crochet project. It will take about 12 hours to make a sample blanket. If you're a beginner, it will probably take you longer. This pattern is easy for beginners, but crocheters of all skill levels can work on it.

Blanket Sizes: **Newborn baby size.**

Hook: **J-10.**

Yarn: **3 colors of 4 ply worsted weight yarn.**

Other Materials: **Tapestry needle, safety pin.**

*Crochet a Gauge Swatch:*

**Stitch gauge:** 4 stitches = 1 inch.

Especially if you're a beginner, it is best to practice the stitches by crocheting a gauge swatch. Start by crocheting a chain of 25 stitches and follow the blanket instructions listed below until the piece is square. Measure your swatch to confirm how many stitches per inch you are crocheting. If it is 4 stitches for every inch, the yarn and hook you're using is correct and you can carry on from there. If it isn't, you may wish to change the equipment to make sure the end result is what you want.

## *Pattern Instructions*

Make a slip knot and chain 105 stitches.

**Row 1:**

- Put a safety pin or stitch marker in the first chain from hook.

- Then single crochet in the 3rd chain from your hook.

- Chain 1, skip the next chain, single crochet in the next chain – repeat this across the row.

- Chain 1 and then turn your work.

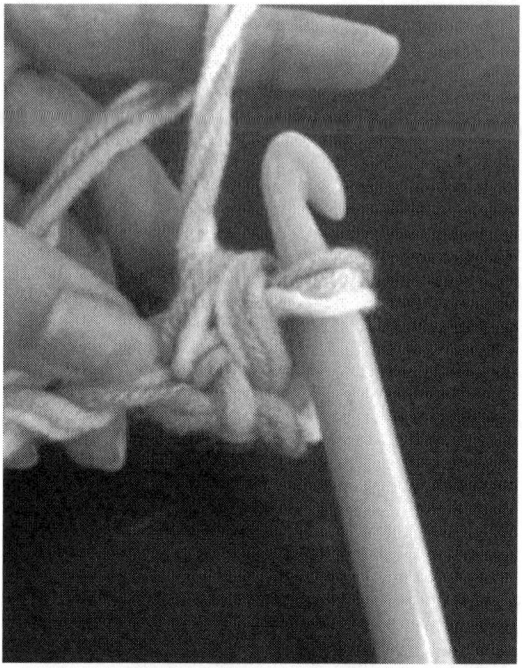

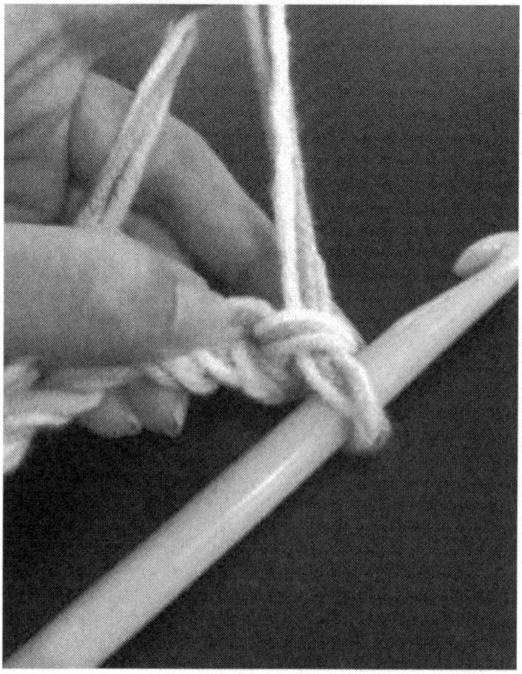

# CROCHET AFGHANS

**Row 2:**

- Single crochet in the next chain- 1 space (the space formed when you crocheted a chain stitch in the previous row), then repeat this pattern across the rest of the row.

- At the end of the row, single crochet stitch into the stitch where you placed the marker or safety pin (remove the marker before making the stitch).

- Chain 1 and turn your work.

**Row 3 and Up:** The rest of the rows are same as row 2, with one minor difference: at the end of the row work last single crochet stitch into the turning chain of the previous row. Continue until the blanket is in the length you want it to be.

**Finishing off**: If you are satisfied with the baby blanket length, cut the yarn, leaving a long length yarn.

# CROCHET AFGHANS

# Basic Tunisian Crochet Stitch Afghan

Tunisian crochet is a wonderful way of mixing crocheting and knitting – although don't worry about the 'knitting' element - you only need a Tunisian crochet hook for it.

Hook: *H-8.*

Yarn: *2 skeins of worsted weight yarn.*

Other Materials: *Tapestry needle.*

Gauge Swatch: *8 Stitches = 1 Inch.*

**Pattern Instructions:**

- Make a slip knot and chain 105 stitches.

- Yarn over and pull up a loop. You now have 2 loops on your hook.

- Keeping all your loops on your hook, repeat the instructions above across the entire row.

- You will end up with 105 chains on your hook. Do not turn.

CROCHET AFGHANS

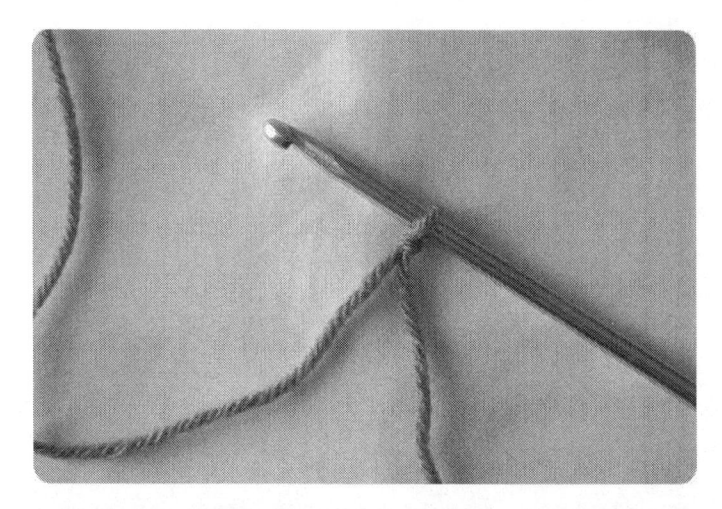

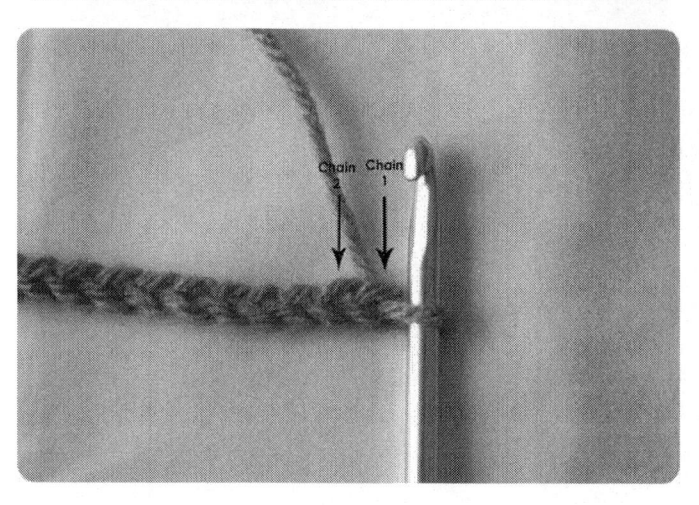

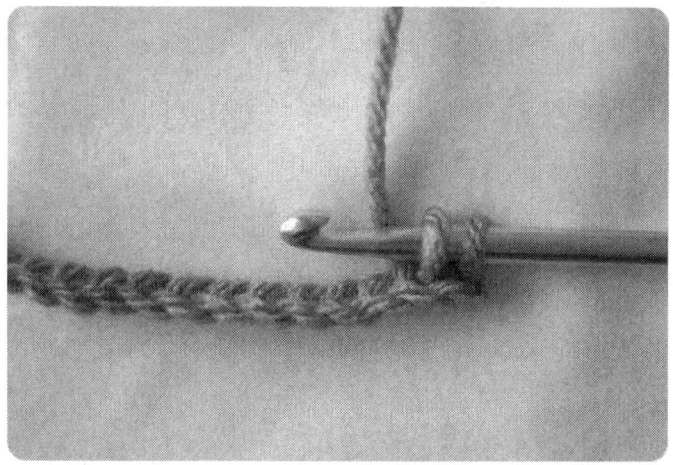

**Foundation Row:**

- Yarn over and pull through the first loop.

- Yarn over and pull through 2 loops. Repeat this instruction across the rest of the row.

- You will be left with 1 loop on the hook.

CROCHET AFGHANS

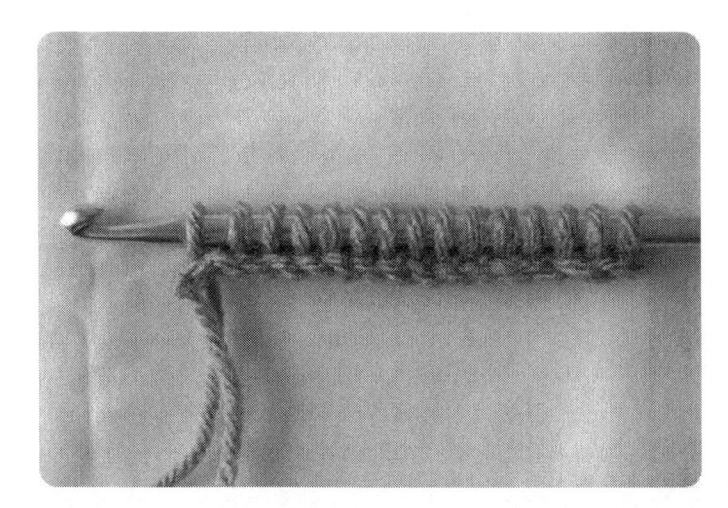

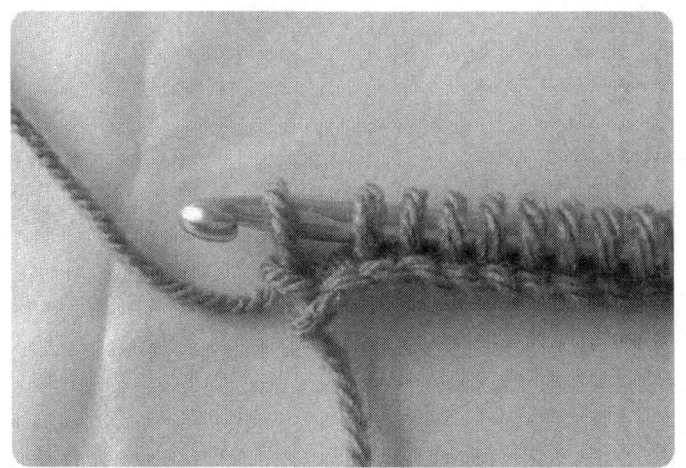

**Row 1:**

In this row, you will be working with the vertical bars created from your foundation row. (Don't forget, there are images below that you can use as a reference point.)

- Skip the first vertical bar from the previous row and insert your hook into the second vertical bar.

- Yarn over and pull up a loop. Now you have 2 loops on your hook. Repeat this instruction until the end of the row.

- Do not turn your work.

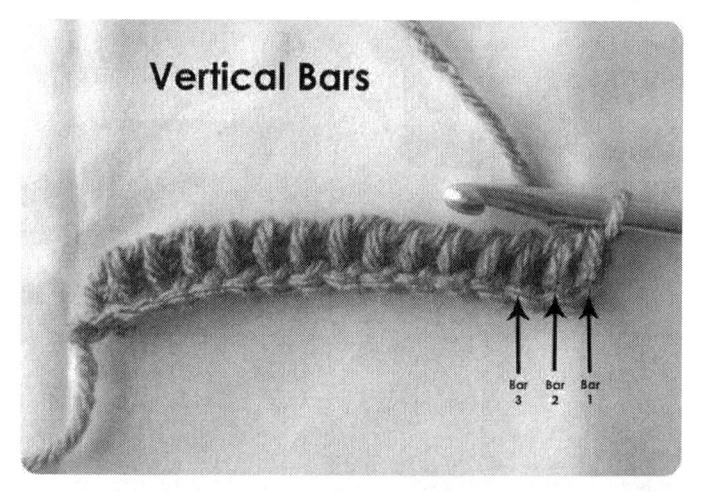

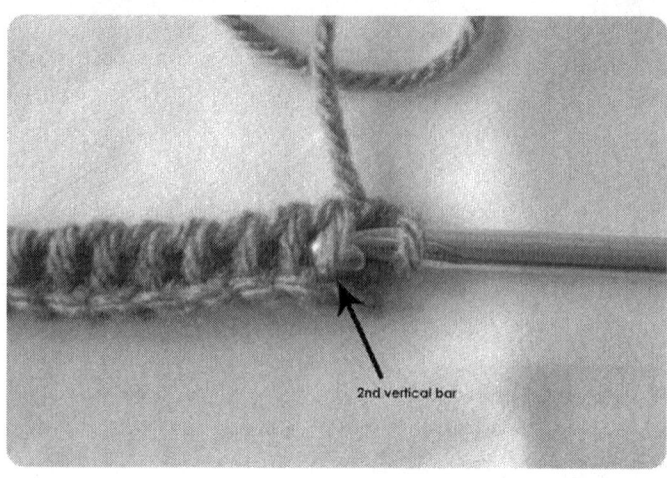

## Row 2:

- Yarn over and pull through the first loop.

- Yarn over and pull through 2 loops. Repeat this instruction across the row.

- You'll be left with only one loop on your hook.

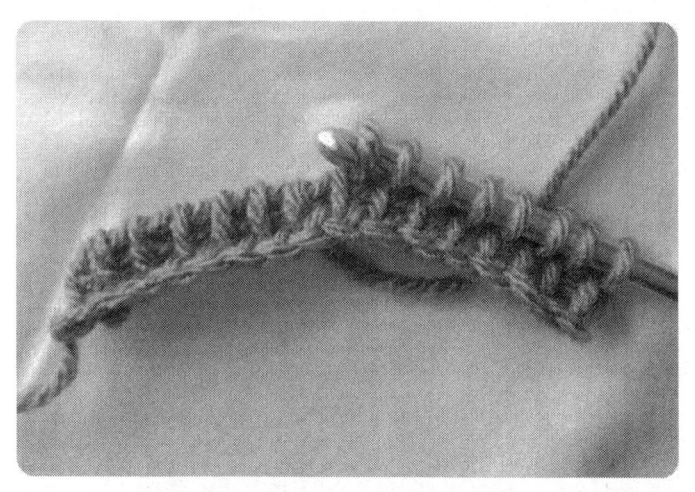

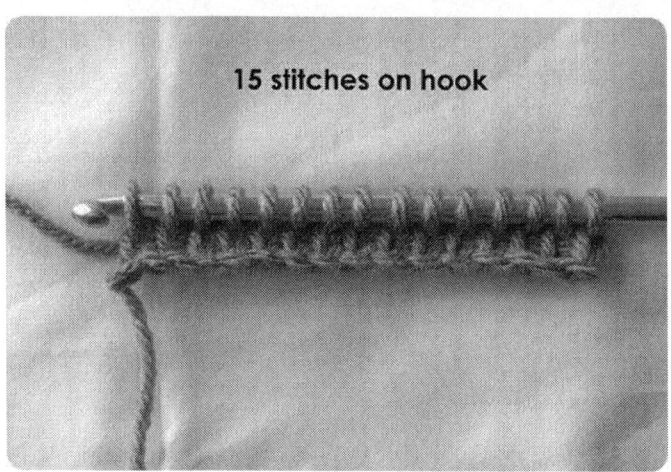

**15 stitches on hook**

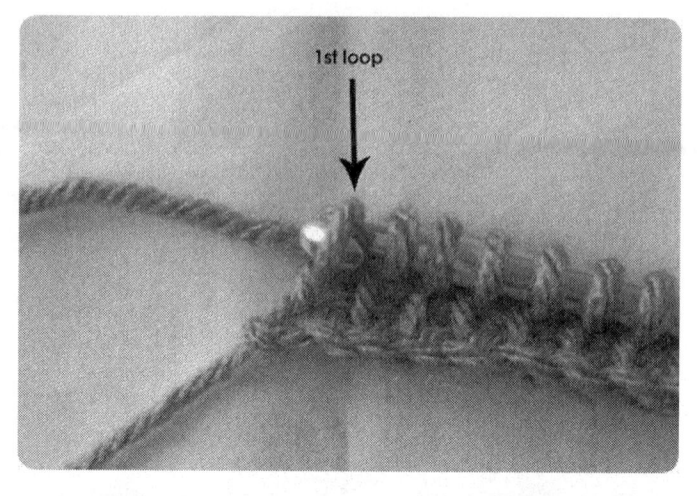

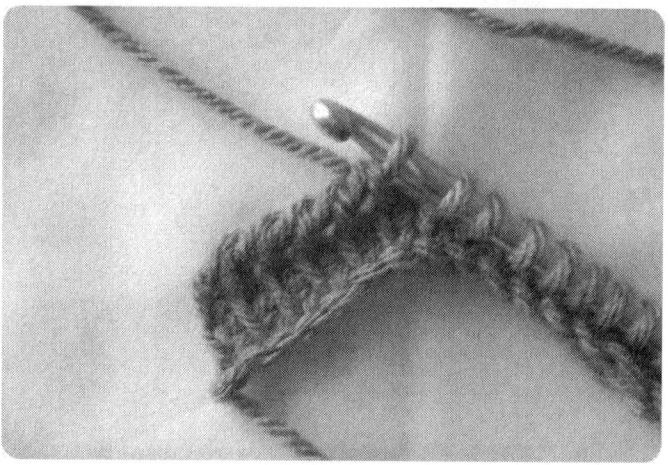

**Row 3+:**

Repeat rows 1 and 2 until the afghan is the length you want it to be. Then fasten and end the project.

CROCHET AFGHANS

***Tip:*** Try to work slowly if possible. That will help preventing your work from curling.

# Basic Yo-Yo Pattern Afghan

A yo-yo afghan gives a unique circular pattern. It's fun and very different so will leave you with a product to be proud of! The pattern is worked in rounds.

Hook: *I-9*.

Yarn: *one skein of worsted weight yarn (approx 62" of yarn needed).*

Other Materials: *Tapestry needle.*

Gauge Swatch: *24 stitches = 4 inches.*

*Pattern Instructions*:

Create a slip knot and chain 4 stitches. Join these with a slip stitch in the first chain to create a ring.

CROCHET AFGHANS

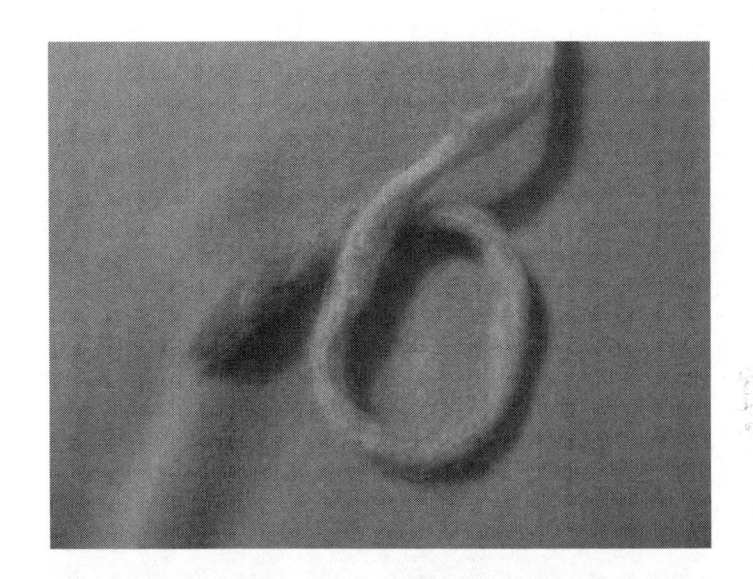

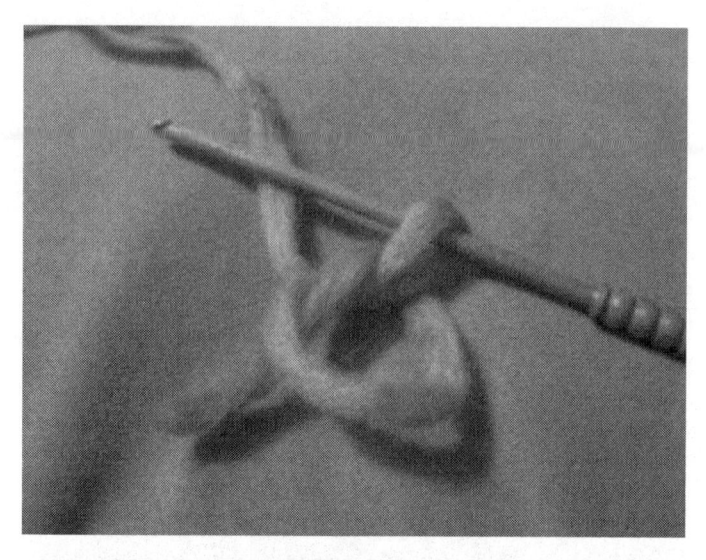

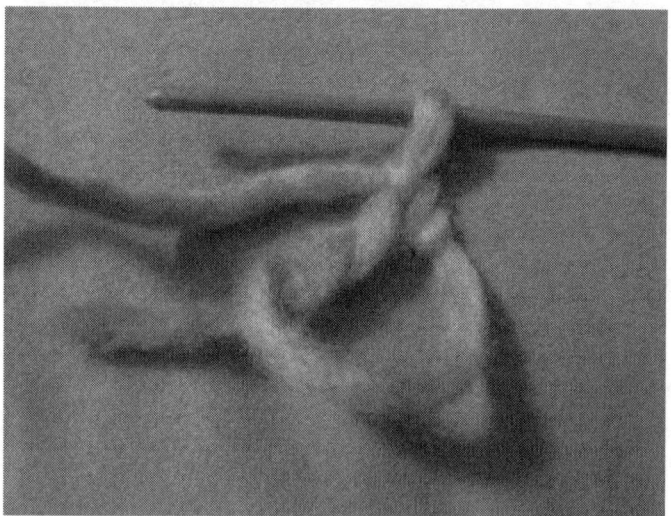

**Round 1**:

Chain 3 as the first double crochet, work 11 more double crochet stitches in the ring and fasten off.

***Flat braid joins method:***

**First yo-yo**:

- Join with a single crochet in any double crochet.

# CROCHET AFGHANS

- Chain 3, then single crochet in the next double crochet 11 times.
- Join with a slip stitch in the first single crochet.
- Fasten off.

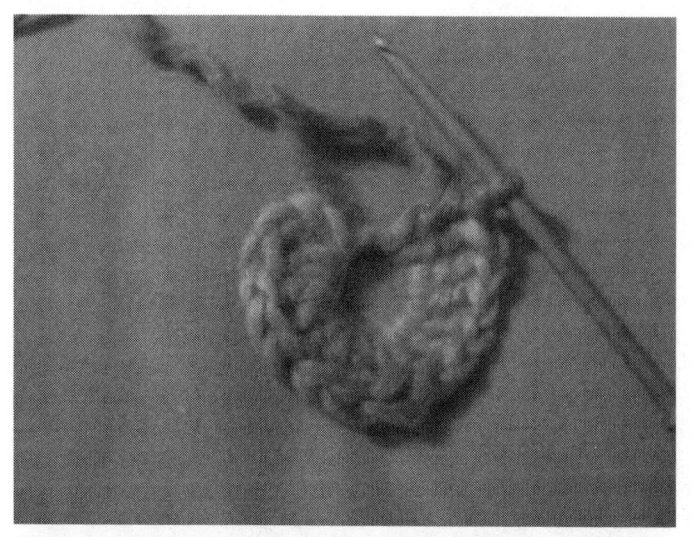

**Second yo-yo:**

- Join with a single crochet in one of the double crochet stitches.

- Chain 3, then single crochet in the double crochet 9 times.

- Chain 1.

- Single crochet (inserting the hook from the bottom) in any chain- 3 space on the first yo-yo.

- Chain 1, then single crochet in the next double crochet on the second yo-yo.

- Chain 1, then single crochet in the next chain- 3 space on the first yo-yo.

- Chain 1, then single crochet in the next double crochet on the second yo-yo.

- Chain 3, then join with a slip stitch in the first single crochet on the second yo-yo.

- Fasten off.

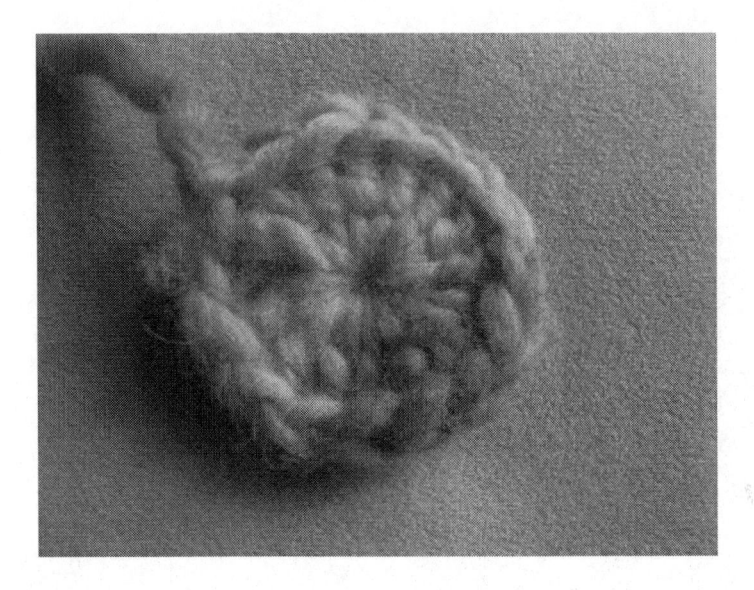

### Third yo-yo+:

Join in loops 1 and 2 as done with the 2nd yo-yo.

# Cables Crochet Afghan

This pattern looks great in any room and can be completed in one color – or a variety of colors depending on your preference.

Hook: *G-6*.

Yarn: *2 skeins of worsted weight yarn*.

Other Materials: *Tapestry needle*.

Gauge Swatch: *4 Stitches = 1 Inch*.

*Pattern Instructions:*

Before starting this pattern, here are the instructions for 2 stitches that you're going to have to complete; the **Front Post Double Crochet** (**FPDC**) and the **Back Post Double Crochet** (**BPDC**):

**FPDC**

Yarn over (wrap the yarn around your hook)

CROCHET AFGHANS

Insert your hook into the front of your work, behind the indicated stitch, and then through your work such that your hook is now at the front of your work again.

Yarn over (wrap the yarn around your hook)

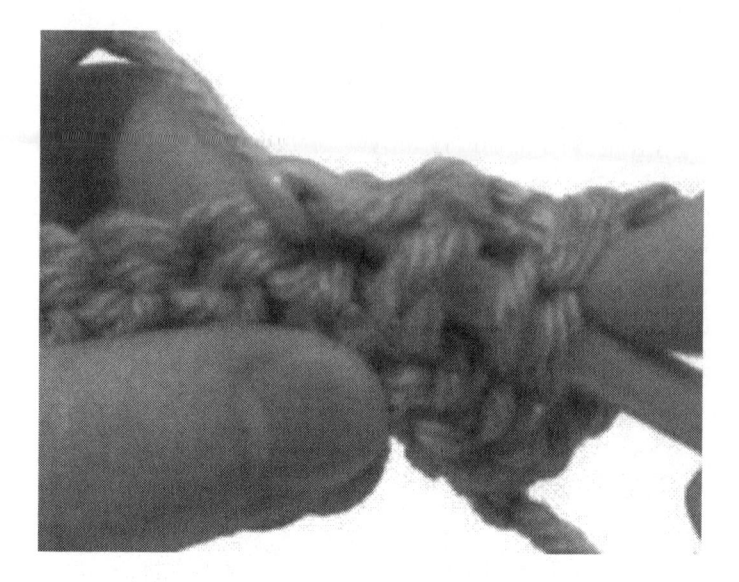

Pull up a loop

Yarn over (wrap the yarn around your hook)

CROCHET AFGHANS

Pull through 2 loops on your hook.

Yarn over (wrap the yarn around your hook)

Pull through final 2 loops on your hook.

**BPDC**

Yarn over just like you will do if you were making a double crochet.

Insert your hook through the back of your work, across the front of the indicated stitch, then through your work again, such that the hook is at the back of your work again. It will look like this from the front:

Now finish your double crochet as you normally would: yarn over, pull up a loop, yarn over, pull through 2 loops on your hook, yarn over, pull through the final 2 loops on your hook.

*Pattern:*

Make a slip knot and chain 61 stitches.

**Row 1:**

Single crochet in the second chain from the hook, then all the way across.

**Row 2:**

- Chain 2 stitches (which will count as the first half-double crochet).
- Half-double crochet in the next 4 stitches.
- FPDC in the next stitch, then cable the next 4 stitches, FPDC in the next stitch and half-double crochet in the next 5 stitches – repeat this instruction 4 times.

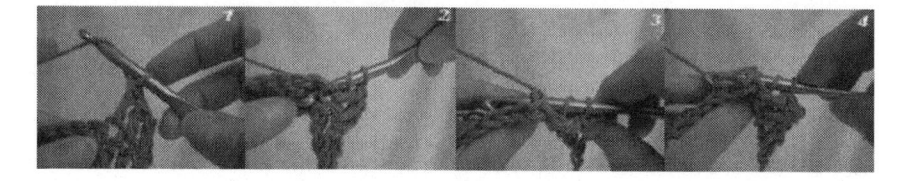

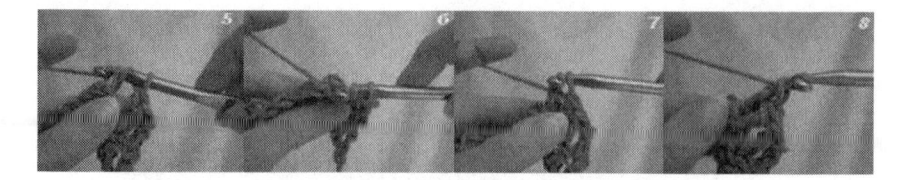

## Row 3:

- Chain 2 stitches and half-double crochet in the next 4 stitches.

- Back Post Double Crochet (BPDC) in the next stitch, cable the following 4 stitches, BPDC in the next stitch and half-double crochet the next 5 stitches – repeat this 4 times.

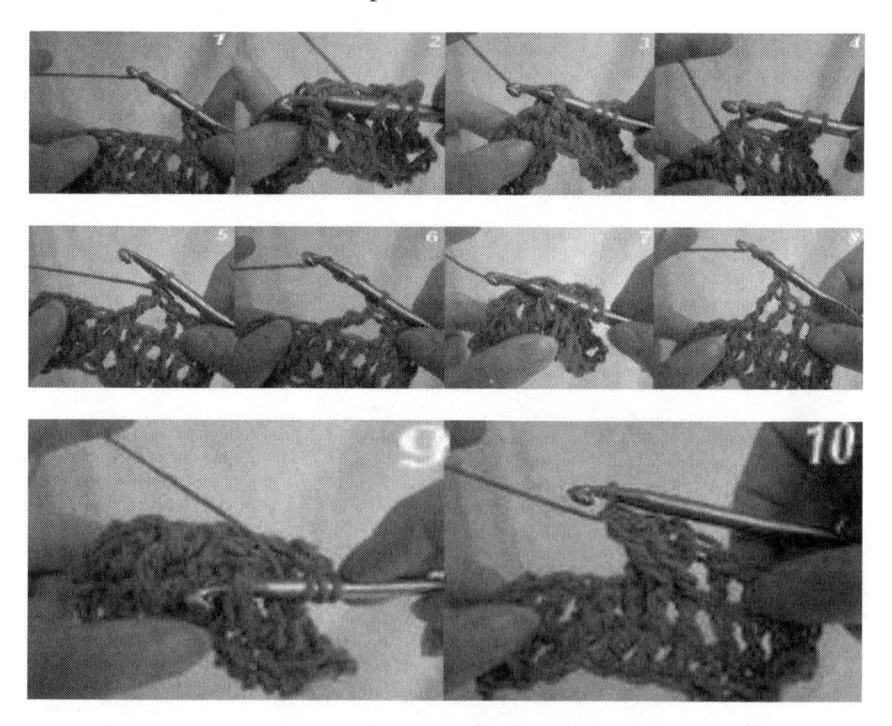

## Row 4:

Repeat rows 2 and 3 until the blanket is the length you want it, then fasten off.

CROCHET AFGHANS

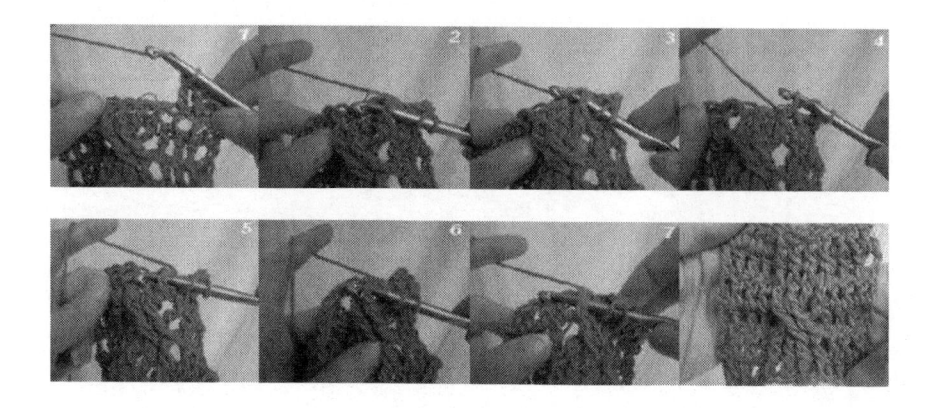

# Easy Openwork Crochet Pattern

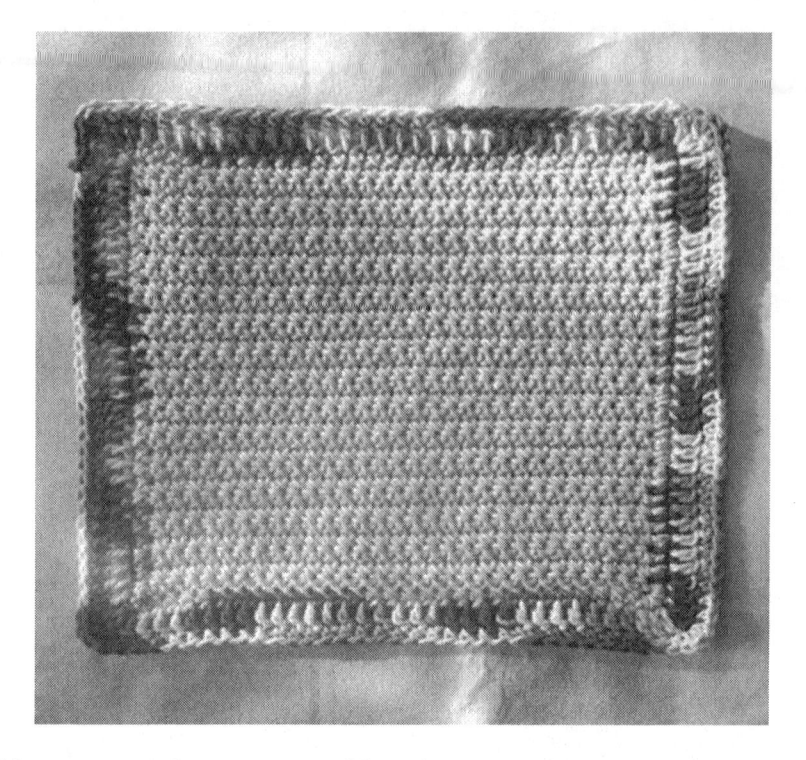

This pattern produces a pretty afghan that can be matched with any decor. It can be a perfect gift for any occasion.

Blanket Size: **44" by 54'**.

Hook: **K-10**.

Yarn: **6 skeins (Lions Brand Homespun Sierra is preferred)**.

Other Materials: **Tapestry needle**.

Gauge Size: **10 sts = 10 cm, 8 rows = 13cm**.

**Pattern Instructions:**

**Foundation Row:**

Working on the right side, single crochet in the 2nd chain from the hook.

Chain across until you've made 101 stitches. Turn your work.

**Row 1:**

- Chain 4 stitches, then treble crochet in the next stitch.

- Chain 2, miss out the next stitch, then work 1 half double crochet, 1 double crochet, 3 single crochet stitches, chain 2, miss a stitch, 1 double crochet and 1 half-double crochet – repeat until the last 2 stitches.

- Treble crochet in the last 2 single crochet stitches.

- Turn your work.

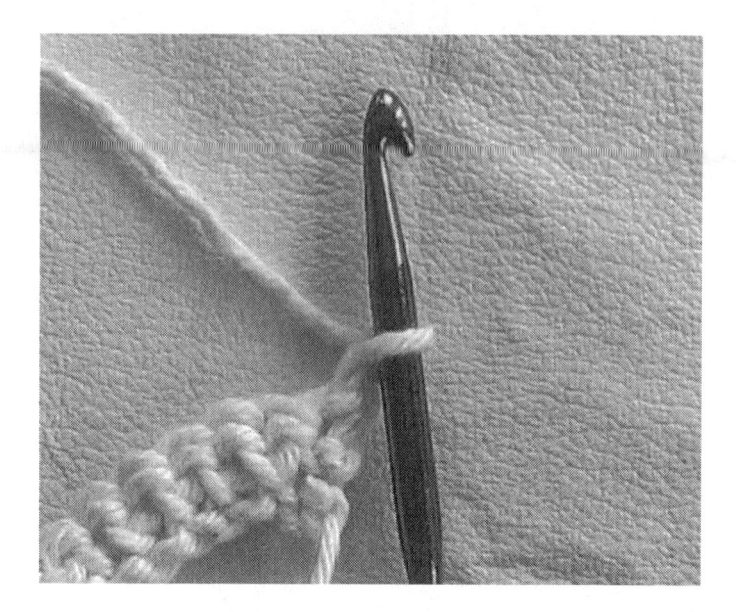

**Row 2:**

- Chain 1 and single crochet in the first 2 treble crochet stitches.

- *2 single crochet in the next chain- 2 spaces, single crochet in the next 3 single crochet stitches, 2 single crochet in chain- 2 spaces.*

- Single crochet in 3 treble crochet stitches.

- Repeat from * to *.

- Single crochet in the last 2 treble crochet stitches.

- Turn your work.

CROCHET AFGHANS

**Row 3:**

Chain 3 stitches, double crochet in each remaining single crochet across.

**Row 4:**

- Chain 1, single crochet in first 2 double crochet stitches.

- Half-double crochet in the next double crochet stitch.

- Double crochet in the next double crochet stitch.

- Treble crochet in the next 3 stitches.

Repeat row 1-4 then rep Rows 1-2 once more.

CROCHET AFGHANS

EMMA BROWN

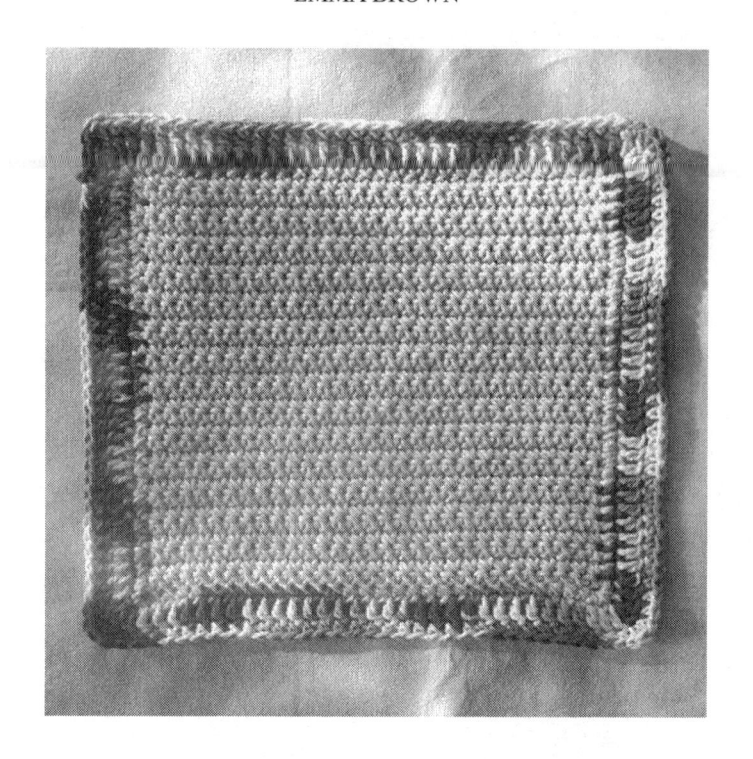

CROCHET AFGHANS

# Checkerboard Stitch Afghan

The checkerboard stitch afghan is suitable for those cool summer evenings. It may not produce the warmest product, but it looks amazing.

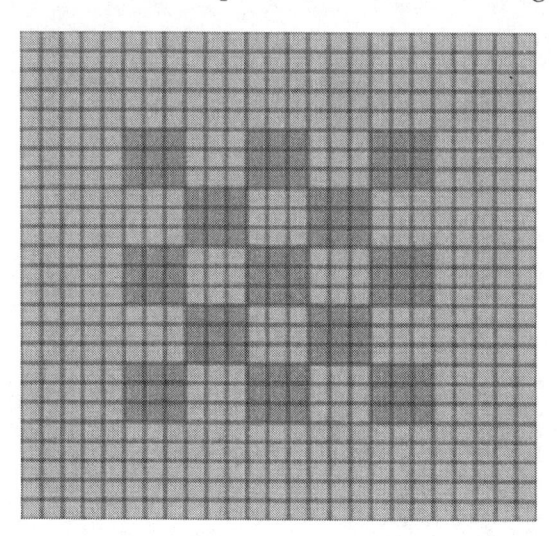

Blanket Size: **46" by 63"**.

Hook: **F-5**.

Yarn: **3 skeins of worsted weight yarn.**

Other Materials: *Tapestry needle.*

Gauge Size: *15 stitches = 4 inches.*

**Pattern Instructions:**

**Step 1:** Make a slip knot and chain 101 stitches. Double crochet in the 3rd stitch from the hook, then again in the next stitch.

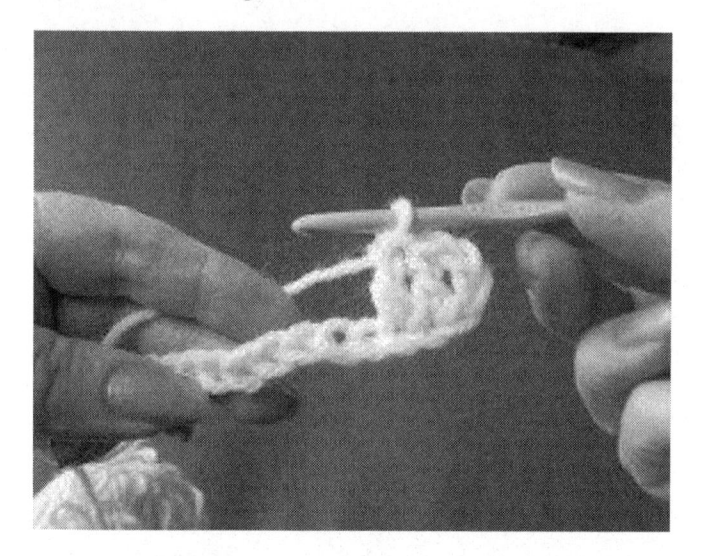

**Step 2:** Chain 3, miss out the next 3 stitches.

**Step 3:** Double crochet in each of the next 3 stitches.

**Step 4:** Repeat steps 2 and 3 across the row. Be sure to finish a double crochet in the last stitch.

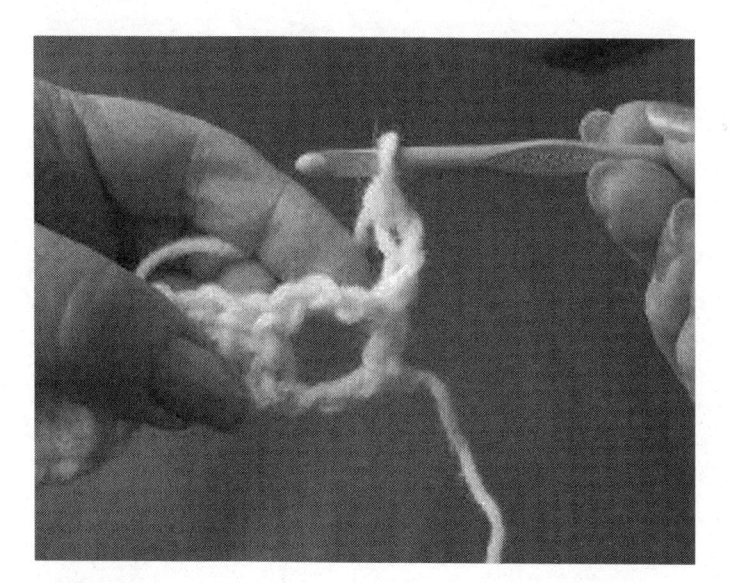

**Step 5:** Chain 3 and turn.

**Step 6:** Create 2 double crochet stitches in the chain- 3 space of the former row. The chain 3 obtains the place of the first double crochet.

**Step 7:** Chain 3 stitches and 3 double crochet in the chain- 3 space of the earlier row.

CROCHET AFGHANS

**Step 8:** Repeat step 6 across the row.

**Step 9:** Repeat all the above steps until the afghan is your desired length.

**Step 10:** Finish off.

CROCHET AFGHANS

# Striped Checkerboard Baby Afghan Square

Add a funky twist to your checkerboard afghan pattern.

Blanket Size: *6 by 8 squares.*

Hook: *I-9.*

Yarn: *Lightweight yarn in 3 colors.*

Other Materials: *Tapestry needle.*

Gauge Size: *4 stitches and 4 rows = 1 inch.*

*Pattern Instructions:*

Make a slip knot and chain 46 stitches.

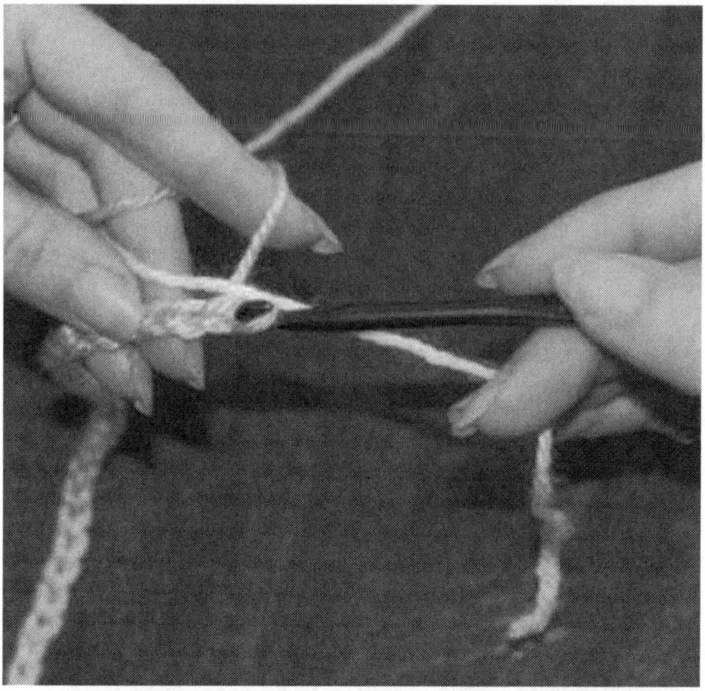

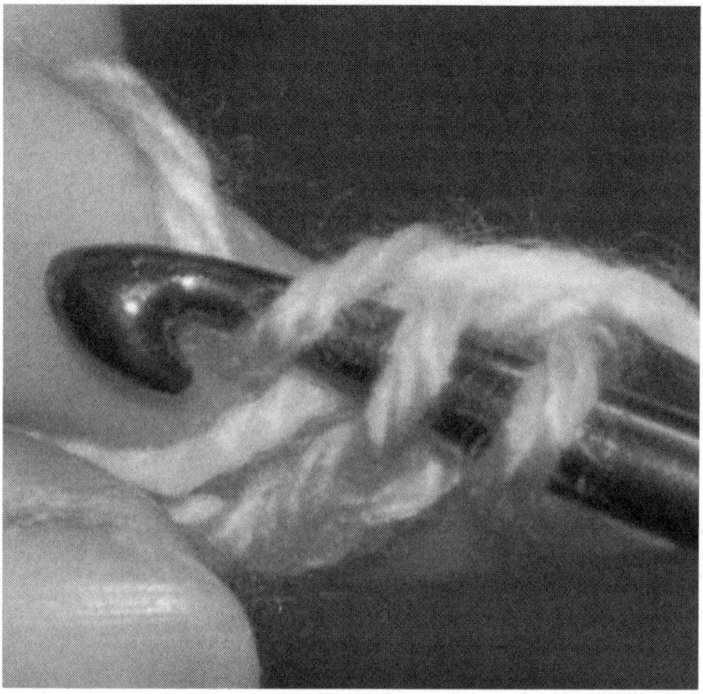

CROCHET AFGHANS

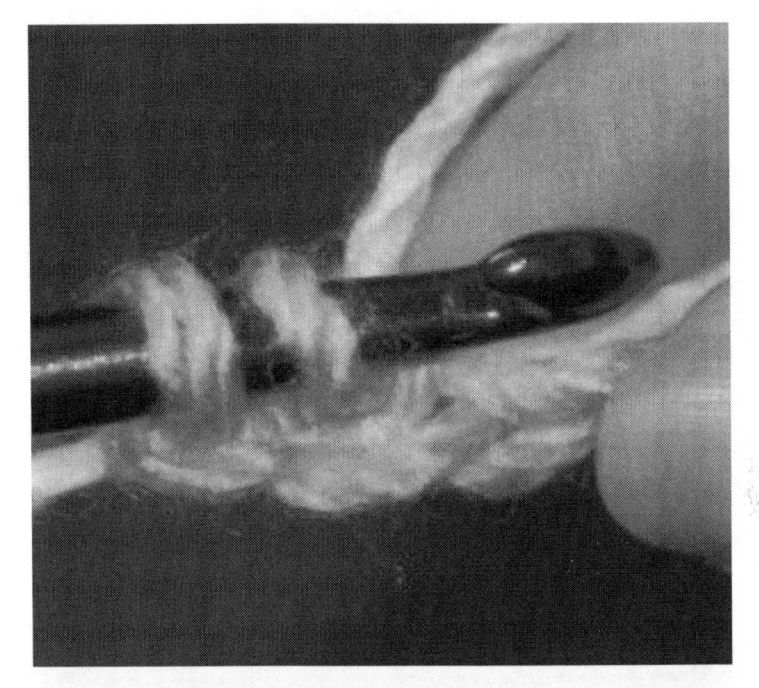

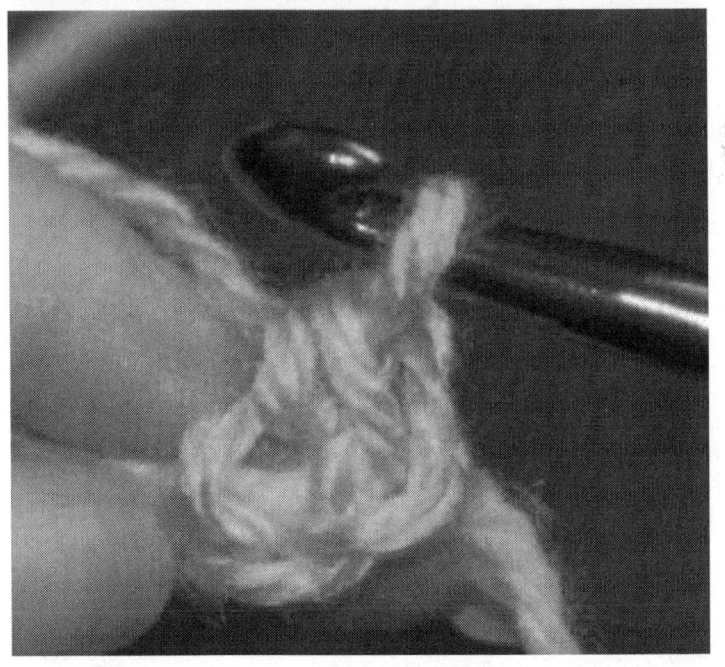

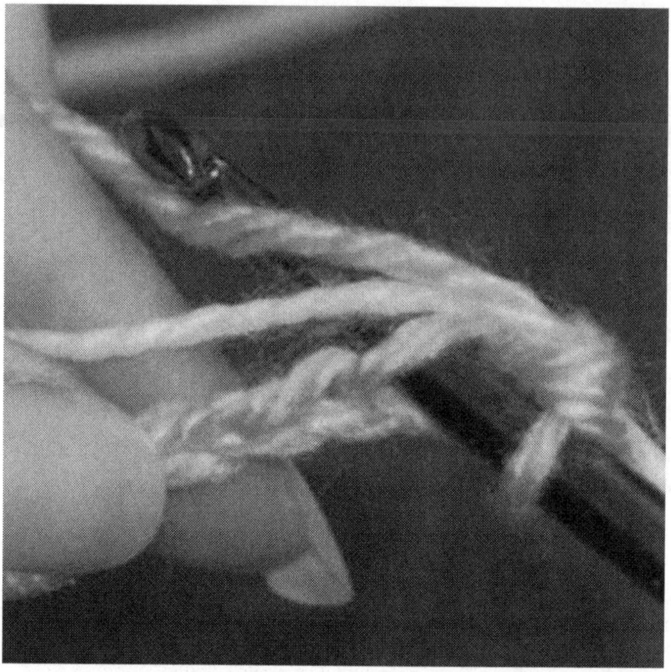

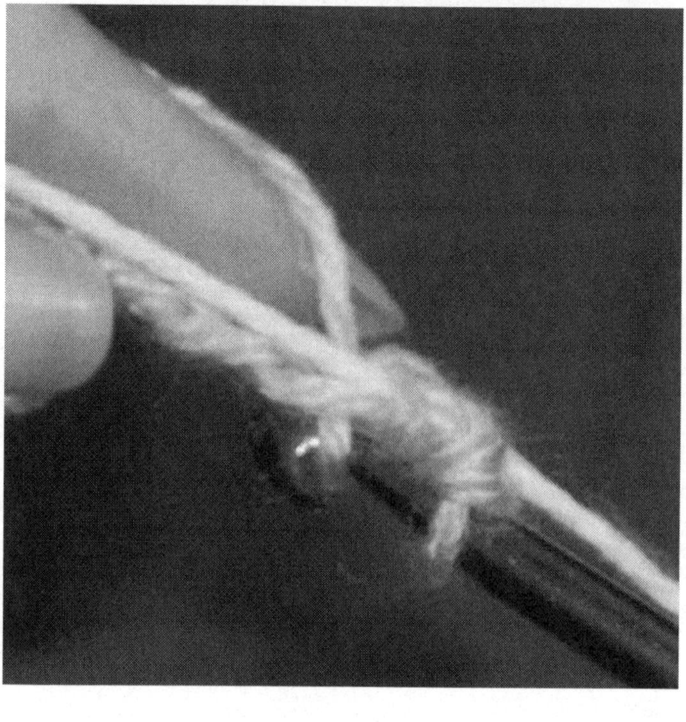

CROCHET AFGHANS

Single crochet across the row, turn your work and repeat. Repeat this until the piece makes a square.

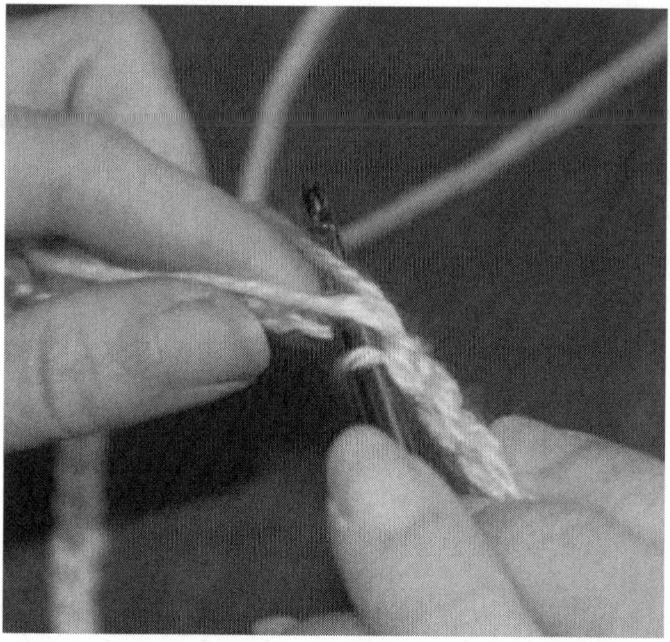

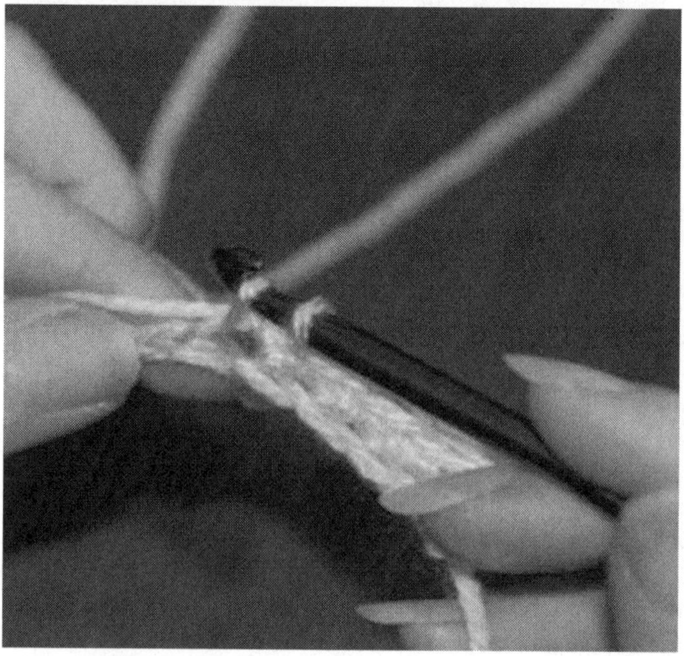

CROCHET AFGHANS

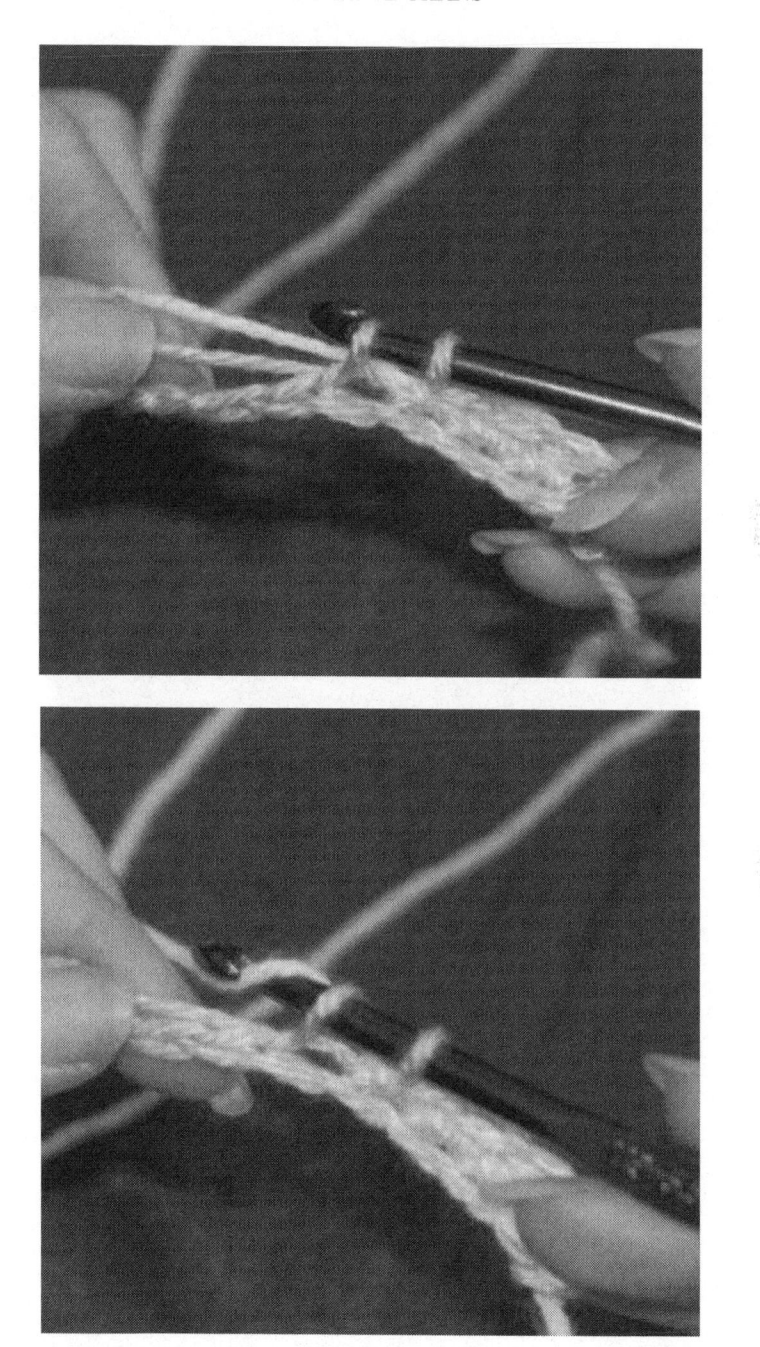

Repeat the steps to crochet this square in alternating colors until you have 48 squares.

Use the whip stitch to sew the squares together.

**Edging for the Baby Afghan Square:**

**Round 1:** Using color A, work evenly spaced slip stitches all the way around the afghan. At the end of the round, change colors to color B.

**Round 2:** Work through back loops only of the slip stitches in the earlier rounds. Work 1 slip stitch in each slip stitch, all the way around the afghan.

CROCHET AFGHANS

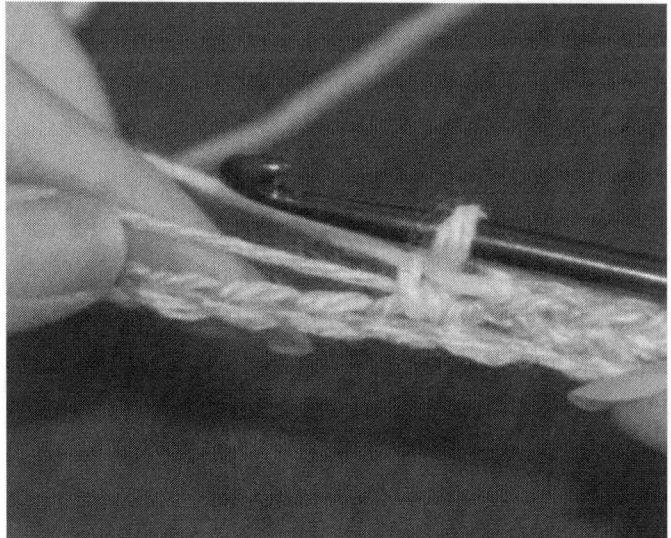

Cut the yarn leaving 6 inches tail before finishing off.

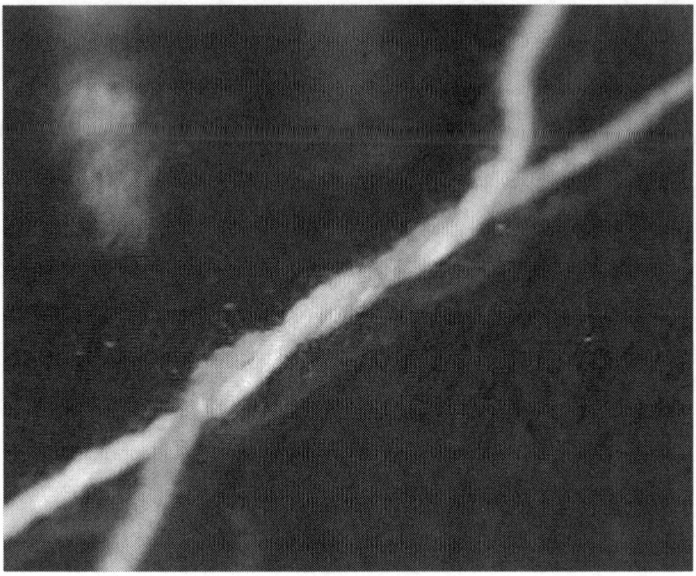

CROCHET AFGHANS

# Intermediate

## American Heartland Afghan

This pattern is more complex due to the design, so is aimed at more experienced crocheters. It is best to practice the beginner ones before attempting a pattern with this sort of design so as not to get frustrated.

Blanket Size: **55" by 70".**

Hook: **J-10.**

Yarn: **For the exact pattern shown in the image:**

- Red Heart Super Saver Fleck*, 96% Solutia acrylic 4% other

- *Nine skeins Aran Fleck* -4313 (color A)
- *Four Burgundy Fleck* -4376 (color B)
- *Three skeins Navy Fleck*-4387 (color C)

Other Materials: **Tapestry needle, scissors.**

Gauge Size: **15 stitches and 25 rows = 5 inches.**

*Pattern Instructions:*

Make a slip knot and with color A, chain 173 stitches.

**Row 1 (Right Side):**

Single crochet in 2nd chain from the hook, then each chain across.

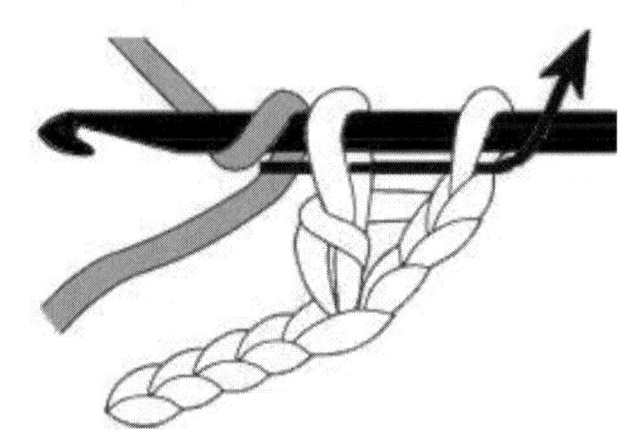

**Row 2:**

Chain 1, single crochet in every stitch across, change to color C at the end of row.

**Row 3:**

- With color C, chain 1.
- Single crochet in first single crochet stitch.

- Single crochet in the next 2 stitches twice, then repeat this across the row.

**Row 4:**

Chain 1, single crochet in every stitch across. Change to color A at the end of row.

**Row 5:**

- With color A, chain 1.

- Single crochet in first 3 stitches.

- Double crochet in the row below for the next 2 stitches, then single crochet in the following 2 stitches. Repeat this across the row.

**Row 6:**

Chain 1, single crochet in every stitch across, change to color B at the end of row.

**Row 7:**

With color B, repeat rows 3, 4, 5 and 2, 3-6 once more. Change to larger hook, repeat again and fasten off.

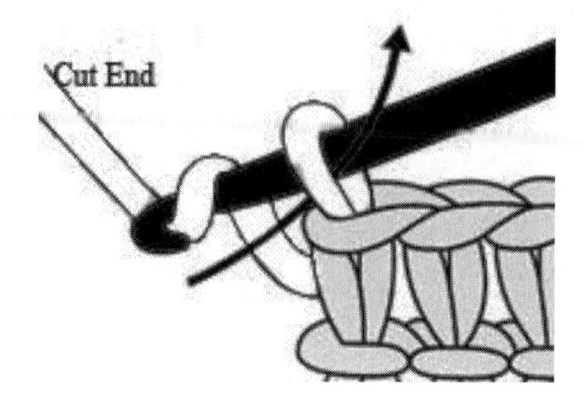

**Finishing:**

**Rnd 1:** With smaller hook and right side facing, attach color C into any stitch and work in single crochet stitches taking care to keep work flat; join with a slip stitch to the first single crochet.

**Rnd 2:** Chain 1, single crochet in every single crochet stitch around, work 3 single crochet stitches in every corner; then slip stitch to first single crochet stitch.

# Basket Weave Afghan

This design gives a lovely thick and warm afghan suitable for adults. Its complex design is easier to master than it looks and once you have gotten to grips with it, you will be able to produce beautiful results.

Blanket Size: **46" by 55"**.

Hook: **J-10**.

Yarn: **3 colors of 4 ply worsted weight yarn.**

Other Materials: **Tapestry needle, scissors.**

Gauge Size: **3 double crochet stitches = 1 inch.**

**Pattern Instructions:**

Make a slip knot and chain 174 stitches.

**Row 1:** Double crochet in 3rd chain from hook, and in every chain across row, then turn.

**Row 2:** Chain 3 for first double crochet stitches, then fasten off and turn.

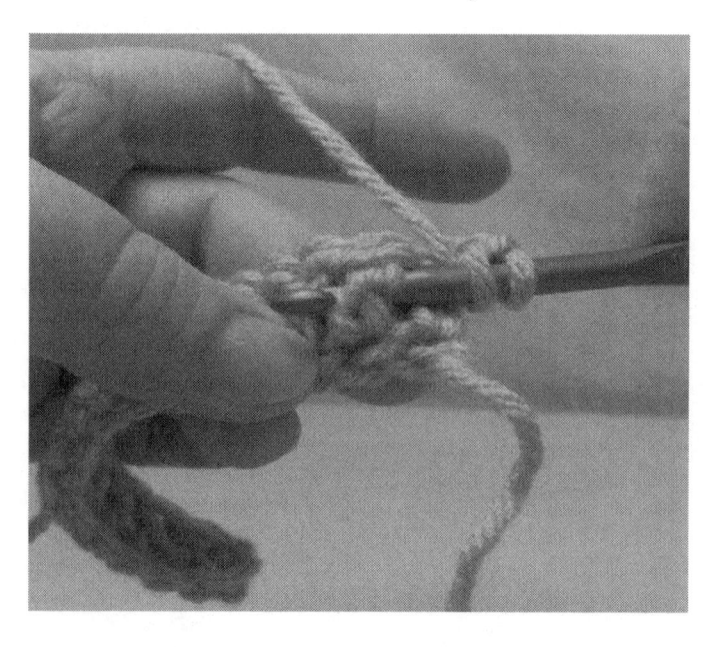

# CROCHET AFGHANS

**Row 3:**

- Change to color B.

- Chain 3 for first double crochet in each of next 4 double crochet stitches.

- Repeat this in the next 15 stitches.

- Repeat all these instructions until the end of the row.

- End with 5 double crochet stitches, then turn.

**Row 4:** Chain 3 for first double crochet, then repeat in each stitch across. Fasten off then turn.

**Row 5:**

- Join Color C.

- Chain 3 for first double crochet in each of next 14 stitches.

- Repeat in the next 15 stitches.

- Repeat all these instructions, then turn.

**Row 6:** Repeat row 4 and end with Rows 5 and 6 using Color A, then fasten off.

CROCHET AFGHANS

**Edging:**

**Rnd 1 (Right Side):** Join color A in the corner. Chain 3 in the first double crochet stitch. Single crochet to the next corner, then chain 1. Join with a slip stitch to top of starting chain- 3.

**Rnd 2:** Chain 4 for first double crochet and chain 1. Join with slip stitch to top of starting chain- 4.

**Rnd 3:** Single crochet in every double crochet stitch and chain- 1 space

around; work 4 single crochet in each chain- 3 corner. Join with slip stitch to first sc then fasten off.

# Granny Square Afghan

The granny square afghan is a very popular design that most crocheters want to try their hand at. Designing each square separately means that you can make the finished product in any way you want.

Blanket Size: **66 x 86 inches.**

Hook: **G-4**.

Yarn: **Medium worsted weight yarn in various colors.**

Other Materials: **Tapestry needle, scissors**.

Gauge Size: **3 double crochet stitches = 1 inch.**

*Pattern Instructions:*

**Rnd 1:**

- Using color A, make a slip knot and chain 4.
- Double crochet 11 stitches on the 4th chain from the hook.

- Join the chain with a slip stitch in the chain at the beginning of the round.

- Fasten off.

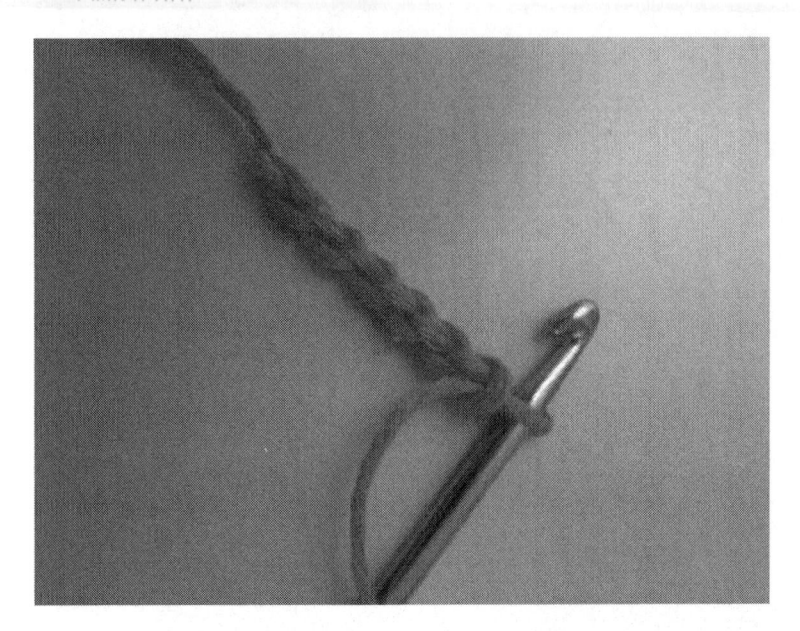

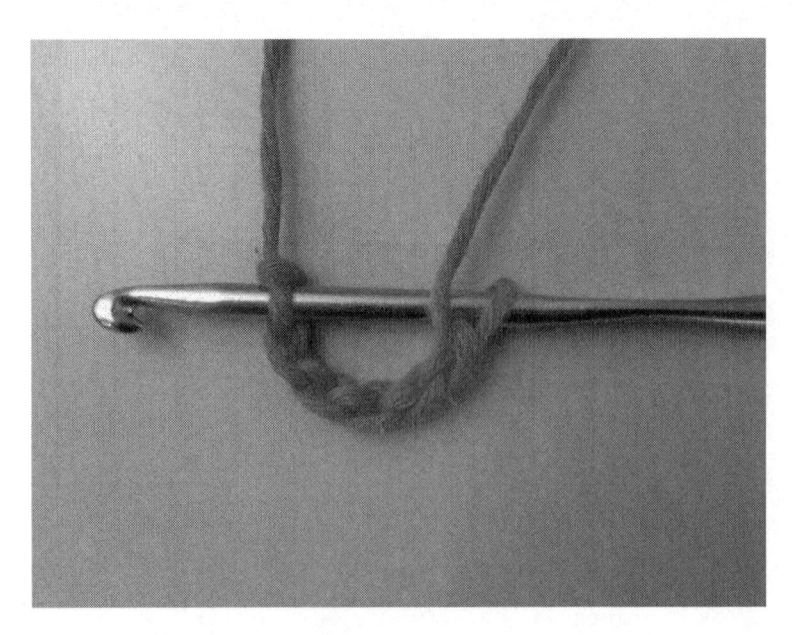

CROCHET AFGHANS

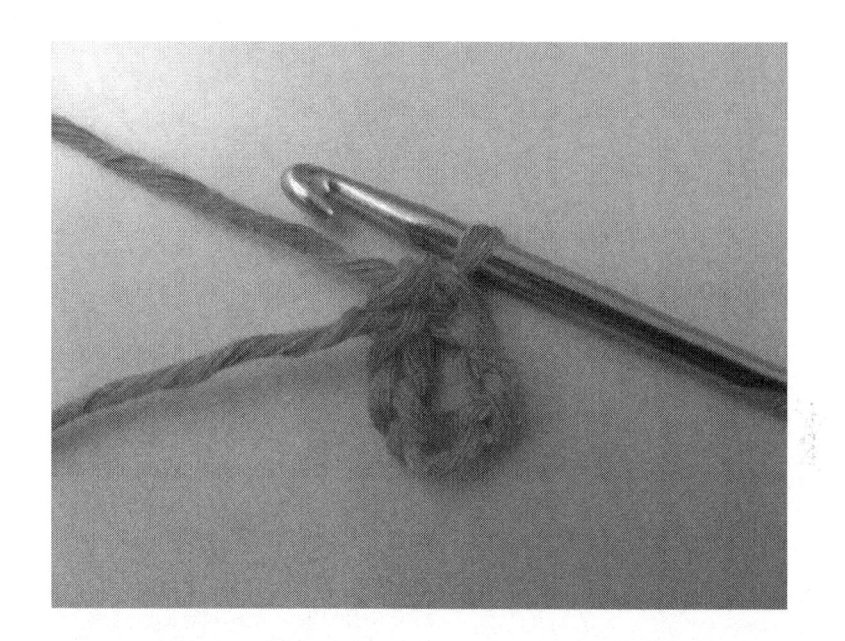

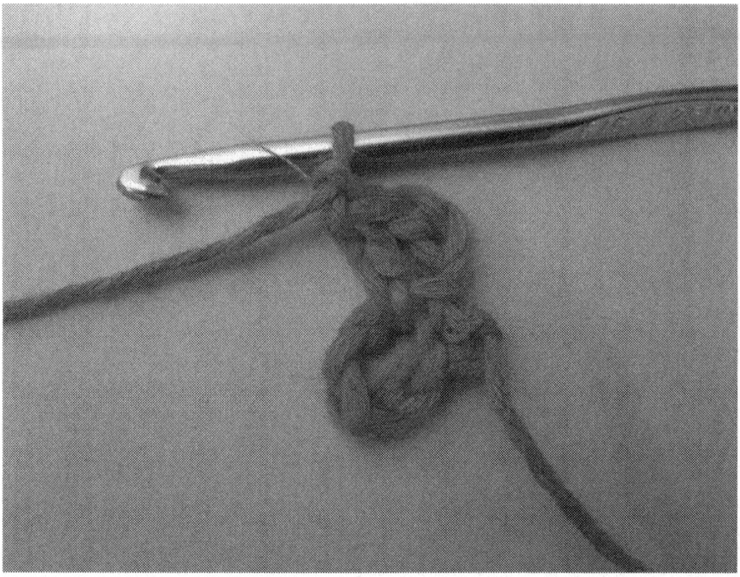

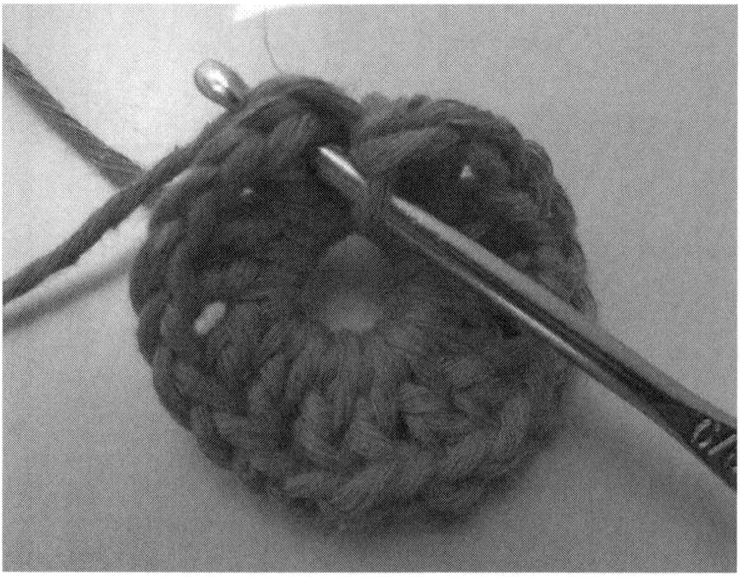

**Rnd 2:**

- Using color B, make a slip knot and insert the hook into one of the chains made with color A.

- Slip stitch to fasten the new yarn to the round.

- Chain 2.

- Double crochet into the same stitch.

- Chain 1.

- Make 2 double crochet stitches into the next stitch, then chain 1 – repeat this 11 times.

- Join the chain with a slip stitch in the first chain.

- Fasten off.

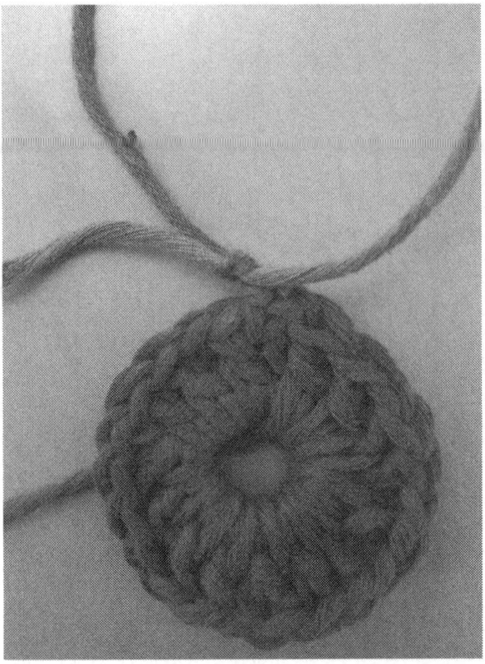

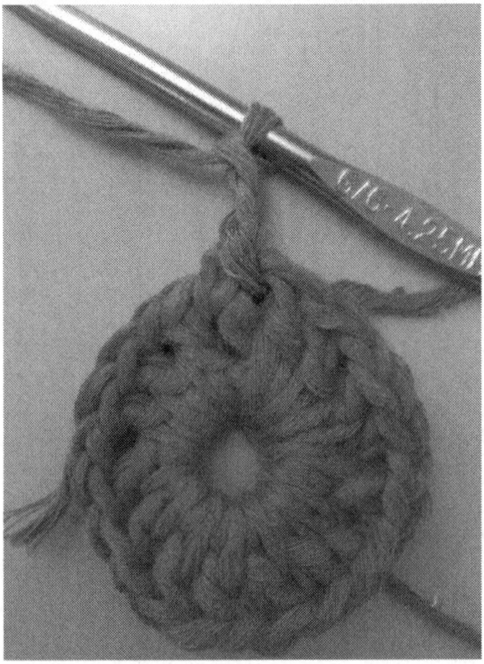

## Rnd 3:

- Using color C, make a slip knot and insert the hook into an existing chain.

- Slip stitch to fasten the new yarn.

- Chain 2.

- Chain 2 double crochet stitches into the same chain.

- Chain 1.

- Make 2 double crochet stitches in the next chain, then chain 1 – repeat this 11 times.

- Join the chain with a slip stitch in the first chain.

- Fasten off.

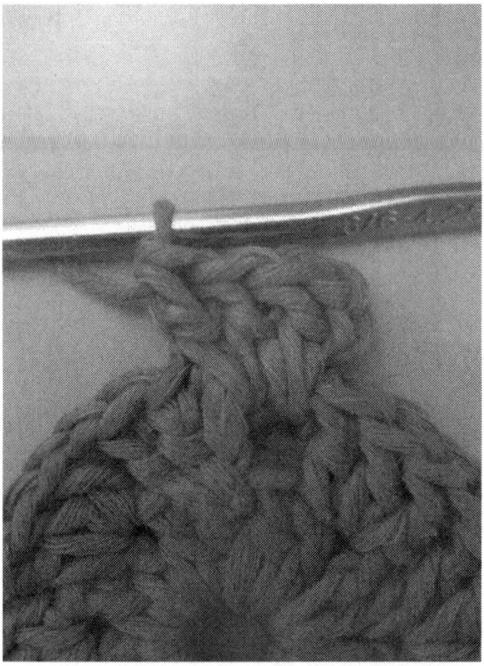

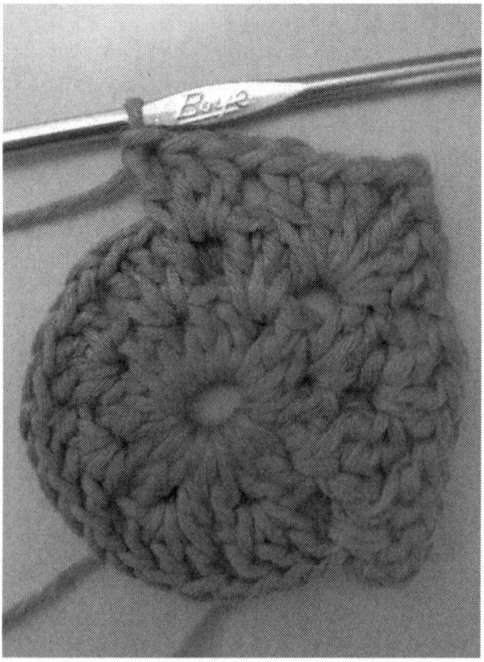

## Rnd 4:

- Using color D, make a slip knot and insert the hook into an existing chain.

- Slip stitch to fasten the new yarn.

- Chain 3.

- 1 Granny Cluster (3 double crochet stitches in the next chain, then chain 1).

- 1 Granny Corner (3 double crochet stitches in the next chain, chain 2, 3 double crochet stitches in the same chain, then chain 1), followed by 2 Granny Clusters – repeat this step 3 times.

- 1 Granny Corner.

- Make 2 double crochet stitches in the next chain.

- Join the chain with a slip stitch in the 4th chain.

- Fasten off.

**Rnd 5:**

- Chain 3.

- Chain 2 double crochet stitches into the same chain.

- Chain 1.

- 1 Granny Cluster.

- Chain 1.

- 1 Granny Corner, 3 Granny Clusters – repeat 3 times.

- 1 Granny Corner.

- 1 Granny Cluster.

- Join the chain with a slip stitch in the 3rd chain.

- Fasten off.

**Star:**

**Rnd 1**:

- Make loop and chain 1.
- Work 15 single crochet stitches.
- Join with a slip stitch in the first single crochet.
- Draw loop shut and weave end with a tapestry needle.

**Rnd 2:**

- Chain 6.
- Slip stitch in 2$^{nd}$ chain from hook.
- For sewing leave a long tail - sew star to center of the square.

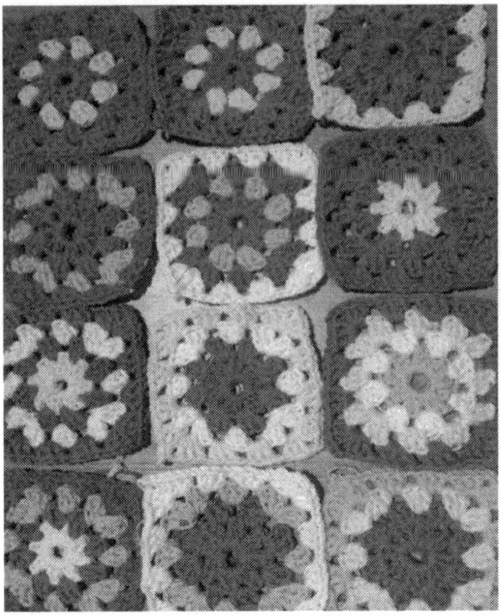

# Granny Stripe Baby Blanket

This pattern shows another way to incorporate the granny square crochet technique into your afghan design to produce a brightly colored, funky blanket.

Hook: *J-10.*

Size: *Toddler.*

Yarn: *Up to 6 skeins of worsted weight in different colors.*

Other Materials: *Tapestry needle, scissors.*

Gauge Size: *3 double crochet stitches = 1 inch.*

### Pattern Instructions:

Make a slip knot and chain 63 stitches.

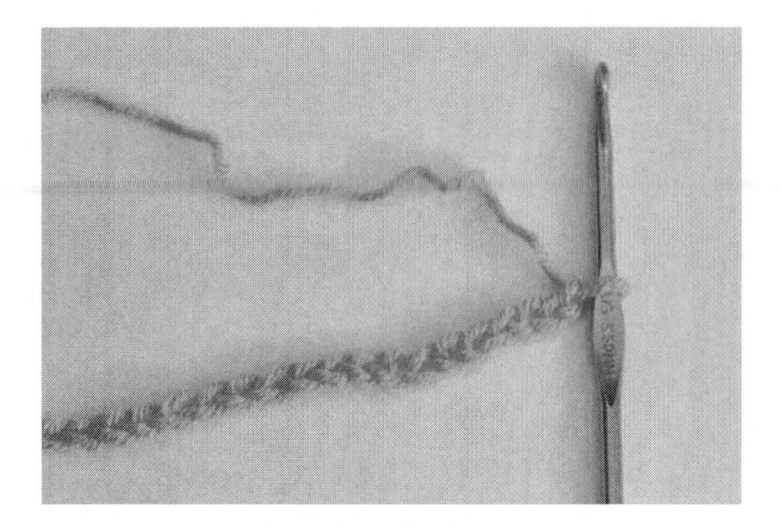

**Row 1:**

- Chain 1 double crochet stitch into the 3rd chain from the hook.

- Miss out 2 stitches, then work the Double Crochet Cluster (3 double crochet stitches in the same chain) – repeat this 18 times.

- Make 2 double crochet stitches in the final chain.

- Chain 2, then turn your work.

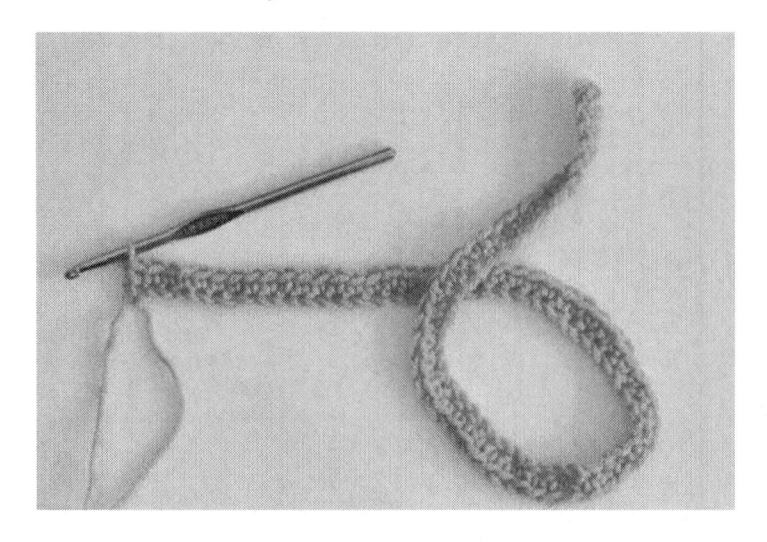

# CROCHET AFGHANS

**Row 2:**

- Work the Double Crochet Cluster into the first space between the Clusters on the previous row – repeat this all the way across.

- Finish with 1 double crochet into the end of the chain.

- Cut yarn and lace ends.

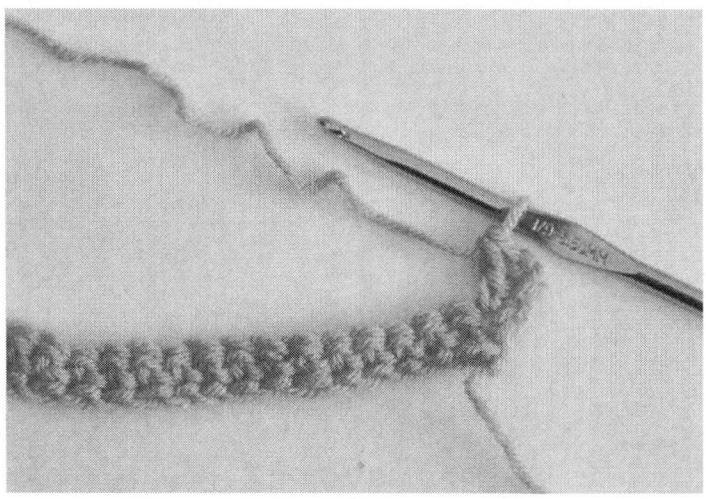

**Row 3:**

- Join a new color yarn with a slip stitch.
- Chain 2.
- Chain 1 double crochet stitch in the same space.
- Work Double Crochet Clusters in every space.
- Chain 2 double crochet stitches at the end of the row.
- Chain 2, and turn your work.

## Row 4:

- Work Double Crochet Clusters in all the spaces across the row.

- Finish with 1 double crochet stitch at the end of the row.

- Cut yarn and lace ends.

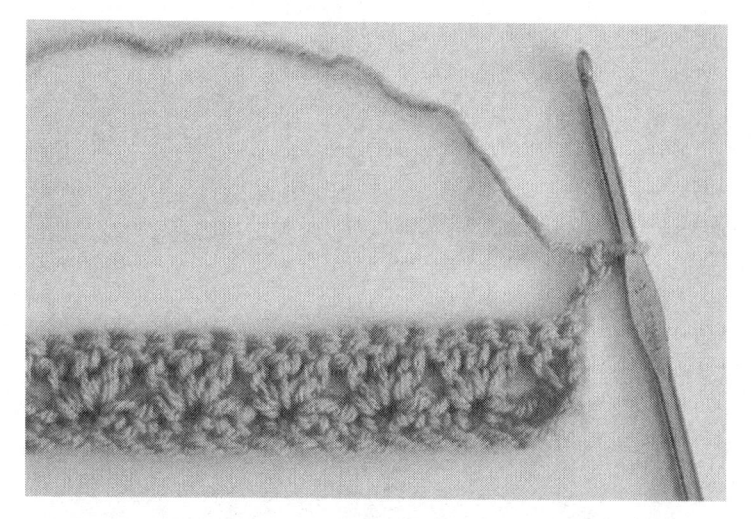

Repeat rows 3 and 4 eighteen times.

## Border:

**Round 1:** Single crochet around the whole blanket working 3 single crochet stitches into every corner stitch. Cut yarn and lace ends.

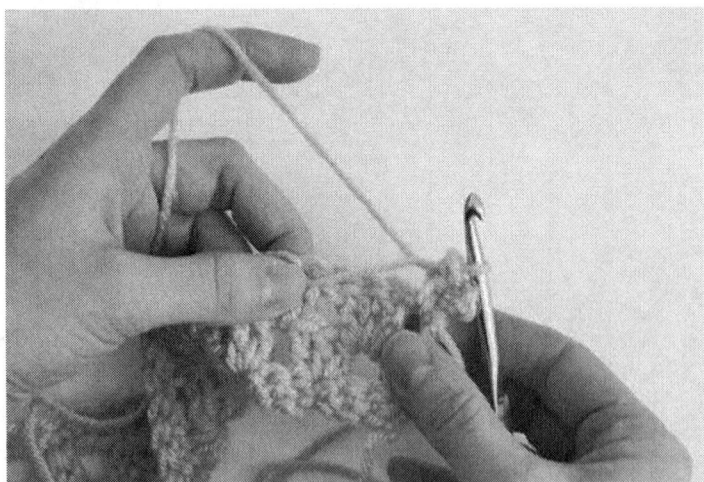

**Round 2:** Change to the 2nd border yarn color you have chosen and single crochet around the whole blanket again working 3 single crochet stitches into every corner stitch. Cut yarn and lace ends.

CROCHET AFGHANS

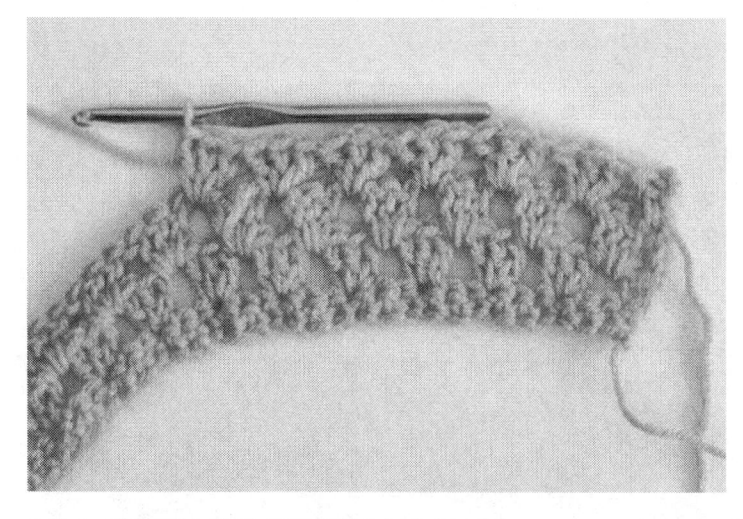

# Granny Ripple Afghan

The ripple stitch is a brilliant design that adds an intricate look to an afghan.

Blanket Size: **53" by 68"**.

Hook: **K-10.5 and I-9**.

Yarn: **Worsted weight yarn. Suggested colors – Rose, Pale Rose, Burgundy, White.**

Other Materials: **Tapestry needle, scissors**.

Gauge Size: **4 stitches = 1 inch.**


*Pattern Instructions:*

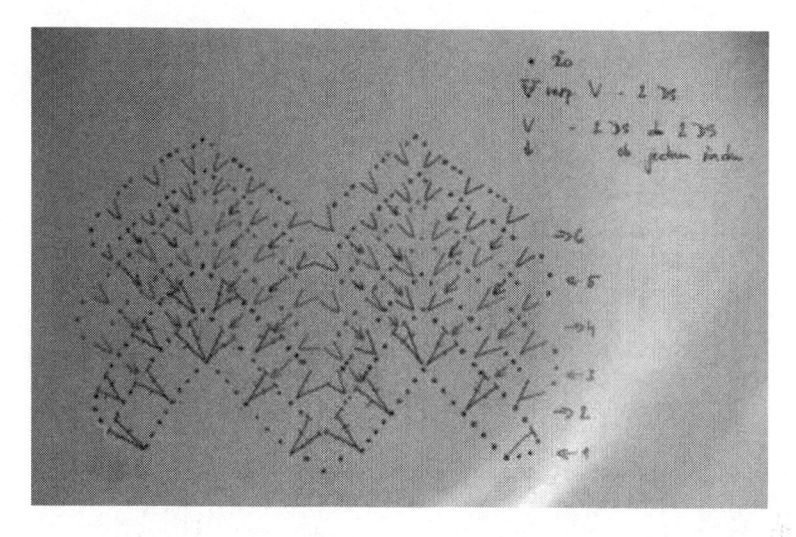

# CROCHET AFGHANS

Make a slip knot and chain 163 stitches.

## Row 1:

- Work the Double Crochet Cluster (3 double crochet stitches in the same chain) in the 6th chain from the hook.

- Skip the next 2 chains, then work a Double Crochet Cluster in the next stitch – repeat this once more.

- Skip the next 5 chains, then work a Double Crochet Cluster in the next stitch.

- Skip the next 2 chains, then work a Double Crochet Cluster in the next stitch.

- Skip the next 2 chains, then work a Double Crochet Cluster in the next stitch.

- Chain 3, the work another Double Crochet Cluster in the next chain.

- Repeat these instructions across the row.

- To end the first row, and start the next, work 5 turning chains and make a Double Crochet Cluster in the space between the first 2 clusters in the previous row.

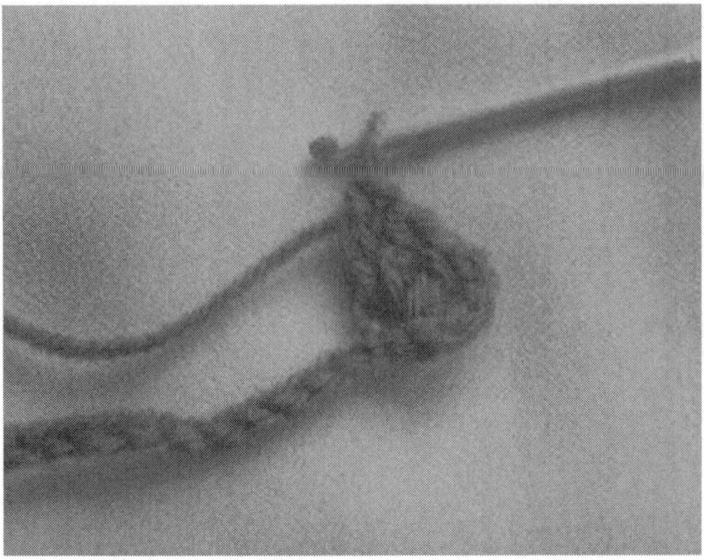

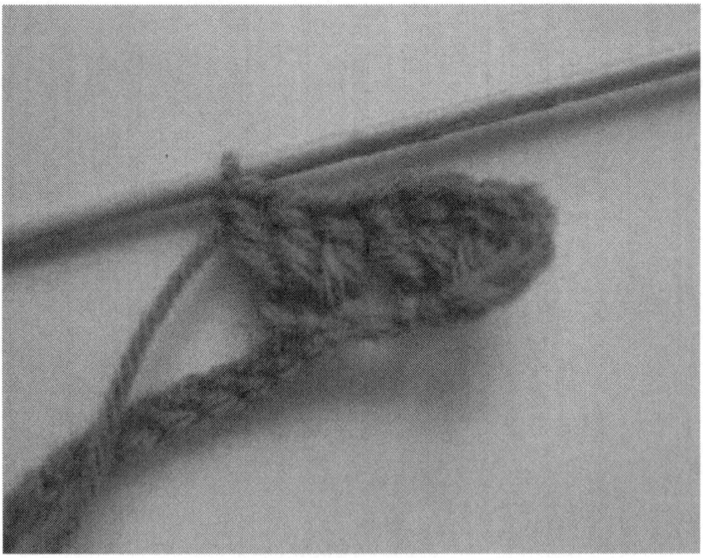

CROCHET AFGHANS

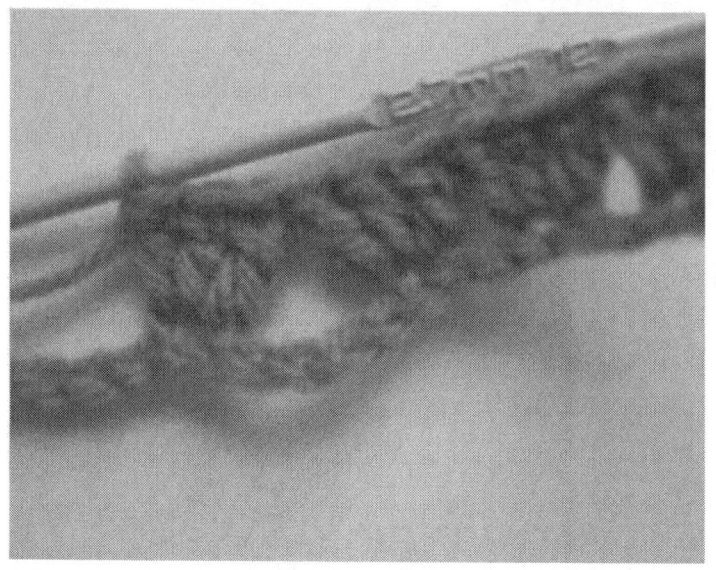

EMMA BROWN

# CROCHET AFGHANS

**Row 2:**

- Work Double Crochet Clusters in the next 2 spaces formed in the previous row.

- Skip the next space (which forms the valley).

- Double Crochet Cluster in the following 2 spaces.

- Chain 3, then cluster in the next space (which forms the peak).

- Repeat this pattern across the rest of the row.

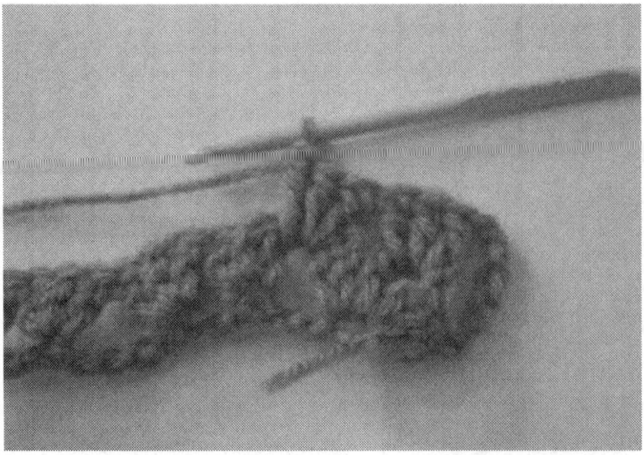

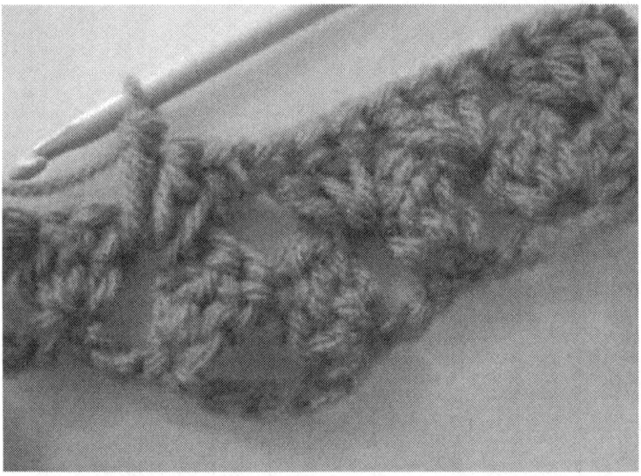

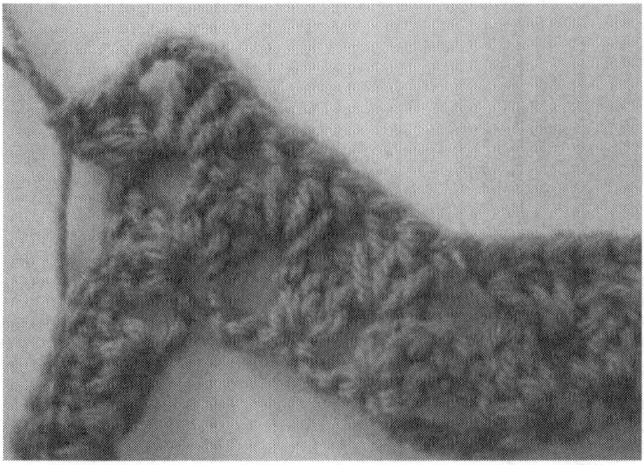

CROCHET AFGHANS

Repeat these 2 rows until the afghan is the length that you desire, then fasten off.

**Edging**:

**Row 1:** With white yarn, work 1 row of single crochet stitches, equally spaced around whole outside edge. Then join with a slip stitch in 1st single crochet. Do not turn.

**Row 2:** Working from left to right, single crochet in each stitch around for overturn single crochet. Fasten off.

# CROCHET AFGHANS

# Lace Afghan

The lace stitch is another unique design to make your afghan beautiful.

Blanket Size: *47" by 56"*.

Hook: *F-5 and Q-19.*

Yarn: *8 skeins of sports yarn in 2 different colors*.

Other Materials: *Tapestry needle, scissors*.

Gauge Size: *5 rows = 5 inches.*

## *Pattern Instructions:*

Make a slip knot and chain 152 stitches using the F-5 hook. (The images below work from a foundation chain of 21 – for an afghan you'll need to make it much larger).

**Step 1:** Single crochet in the 2d chain from the hook and in each chain across.

CROCHET AFGHANS

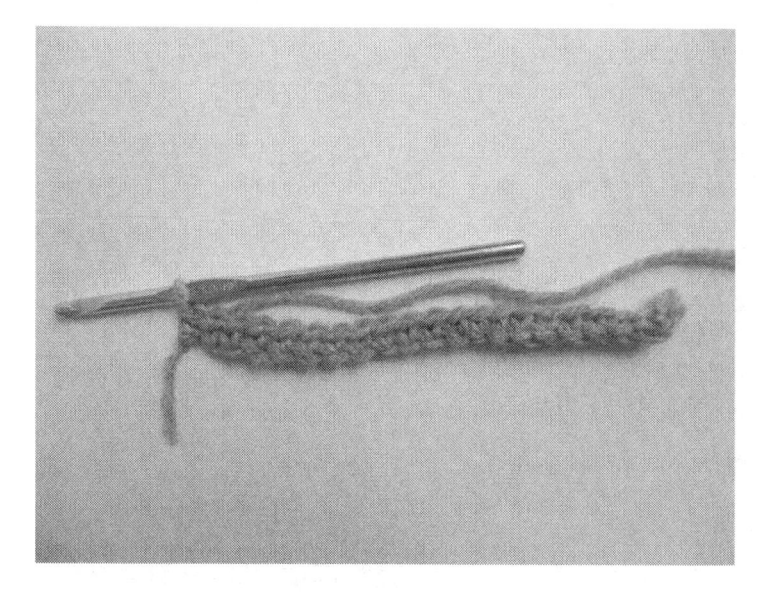

**Step 2:** When you reach the end of the first row, pull up on the loop and slide it onto your Q-19 hook. Slide the loop to the fullest part of the hook.

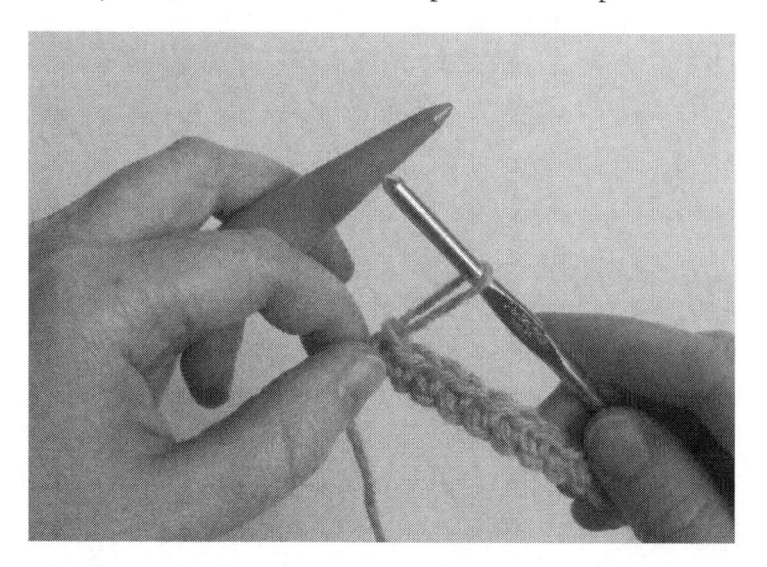

**Step 3:** Pull up a loop from each single crochet stitch in each row and slide it onto the larger hook. (Step 4 shows you how to do this).

**Step 4:** Insert your hook into the next single crochet stitch. Yarn over and pull up a loop. Slide the loop onto the larger hook. Repeat across the row until you have 20 loops on the larger hook.

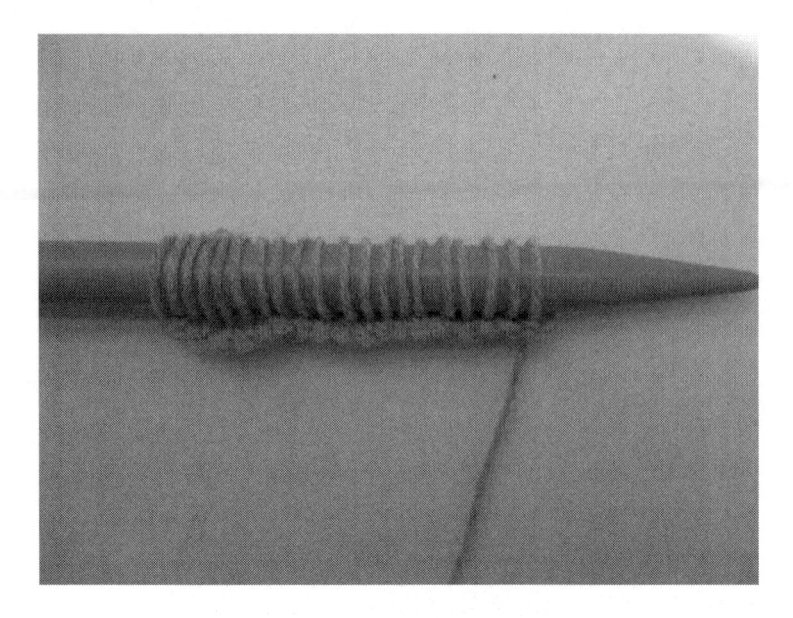

**Step 5:** Slide all of the loops of the larger hook.

**Step 6:** Insert your F-5 hook through the first 5 loops.

CROCHET AFGHANS

**Step 7:** Yarn over and pull through all 5 loops. Then chain 1 for your turning chain.

**Step 8:** Crochet 5 single crochet stitches into the middle of all 5 loops. You've now made your first group.

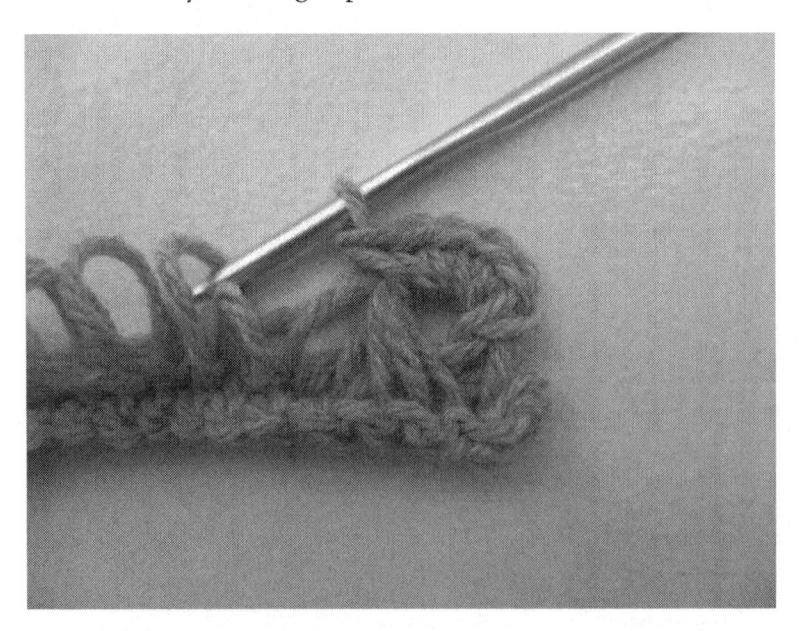

**Step 9:** Insert your hook through the next 5 loops.

CROCHET AFGHANS

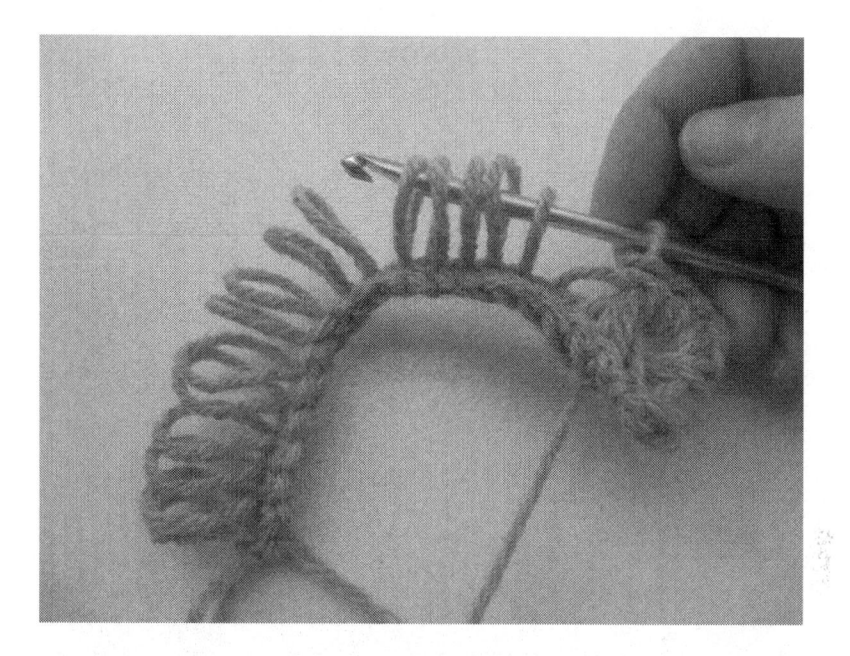

**Step 10:** Pull the loop through and single crochet 5 stitches.

**Step 11:** Continue across the row until all the loops are grouped.

**Step 12:** The single crochet stitches that you've made will form the base for

the next row. Use these to begin another lace row, pulling the loops in each single crochet stitches and place them on the Q-19 hook (as you did before).

**Step 13:** Continue repeating the above steps until you have the number of rows you desire.

CROCHET AFGHANS

# Rainbow Dash Baby Afghan

This gorgeous design is the perfect gift for a baby to keep them warm and looking good during the winter months.

Hook: *I-9*.

Size: *Single bed sized.*

Yarn: *1,200 – 1,800 yards of yarn, preferably in 3 – 5 different colors.*

Other Materials: *Tapestry needle, scissors.*

Gauge Size: *4 stitches = 1 inch.*

**Pattern Instructions:**

Using color A, make a slip knot and chain 92 stitches.

**Row 1:** Turn your work, single crochet in the 2nd chain from the hook then right across.

**Row 2:** Turn your work, chain 3 then double crochet right across.

**Row 3:**

- Turn your work.

- Chain 1.

- Single crochet in the first double crochet stitch.

- Front Post Triple Crochet – FPTrc – (Yarn over 2 times, insert hook around designated post starting at the front, go around the back of the stitch around to the front of the other side of the stitch, draw up a loop, pull through 2 loops – repeat 3 times.)

- Skip a stitch.

- Single crochet in the next stitch.

- Repeat above 3 across the row.

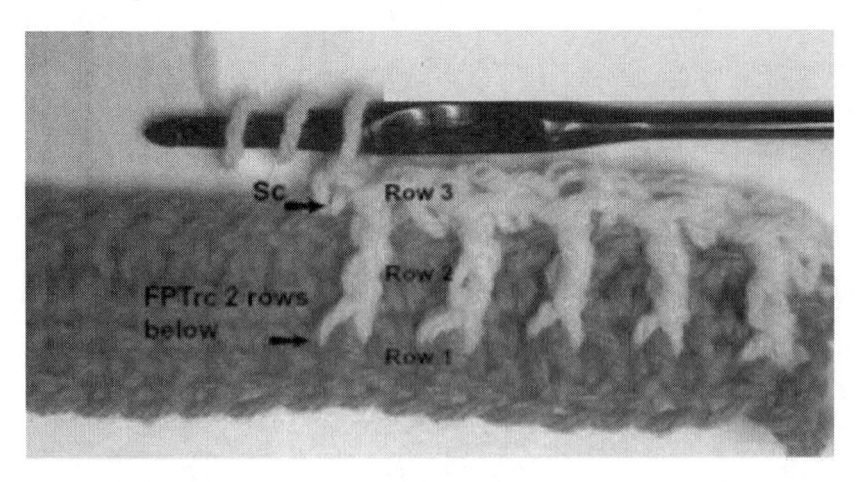

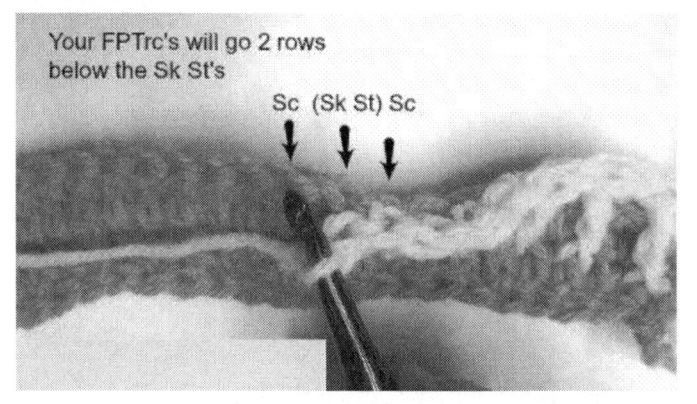

CROCHET AFGHANS

**Row 4:** Turn your work, chain 3 then double crochet right across.

**Row 5:**

- Turn your work.

- Chain 1.

- Single crochet in the next stitch.

- Front Post Triple Crochet.

- Skip a stitch.

- Single crochet in the next stitch.

- Repeat above 3 across the row.

FPTrc around previous row's FPTrc

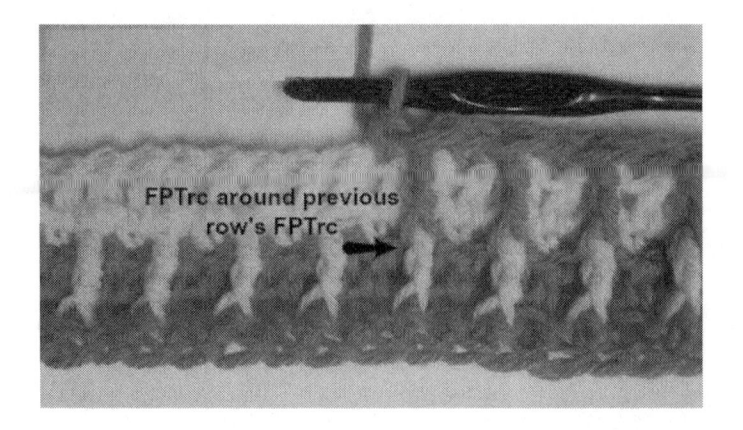

**Row 6:** Turn your work, chain 3 then double crochet right across.

**Rows 7-82:** Repeat the rows above, fastening off and joining new colors with a slip stitch as desired.

*Tip:* To get the best effect from stitching, you should change color in every 2 rows.

## Zig Zag Yo-Yo Afghan

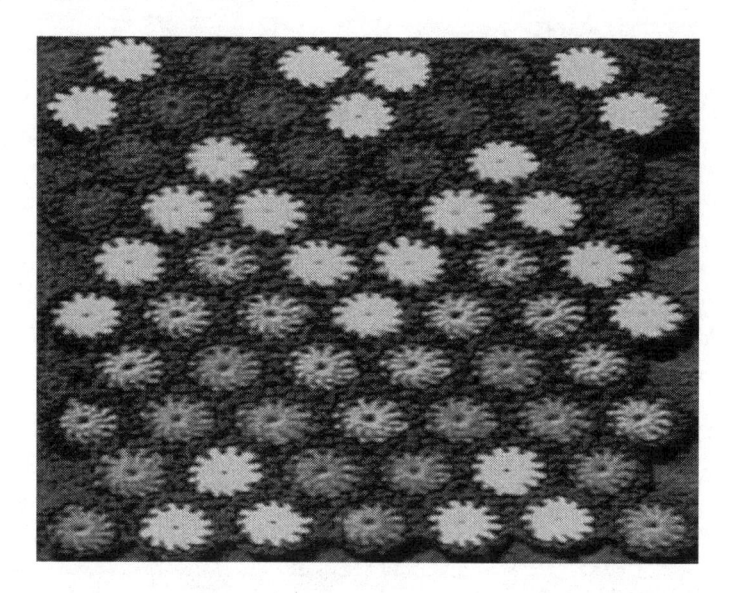

The yo-yo pattern was one that we looked at earlier on in this chapter. This pattern is a more complex version of this if you fancy something a bit more challenging.

Blanket Size: *47" by 63"*.

Hook: *I-9 and J-10*.

Yarn: *Worsted weight acrylic*.

Other Materials: *Tapestry needle, scissors*.

Gauge Size: *24 stitches = 4 inches*.

### Pattern Instructions:

Make a slip knot and chain 4 stitches using the I-9 hook. Join with a slip stitch to form a ring. Chain 3, work 11 double crochet stitches in the ring then fasten off – repeat this for every yo-yo. Standard blanket size suggested in this pattern requires 645 yo-yos.

**Joining Step 1**: Join main color with a single crochet in any double crochet stitch, then chain 3 – repeat this 11 times and join with a slip stitch in the first stitch. Fasten off.

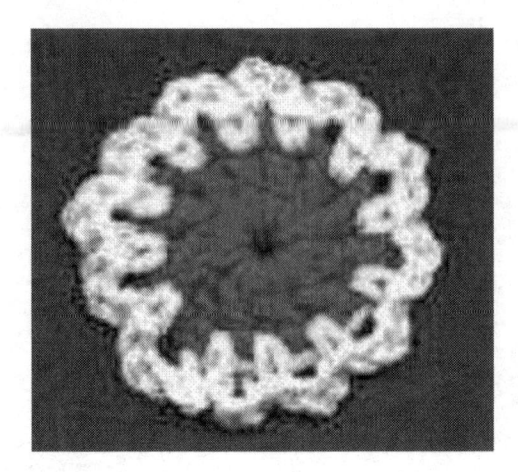

**Step 2:**

- Join main color with a single crochet in any double crochet stitch.

- Chain 3, then single crochet in the next double crochet stitch – repeat this 9 times.

- Chain 2.

- Drop the stitch from the hook.

- Insert your hook through any of the chain- 3 spaces on the first yo-yo.

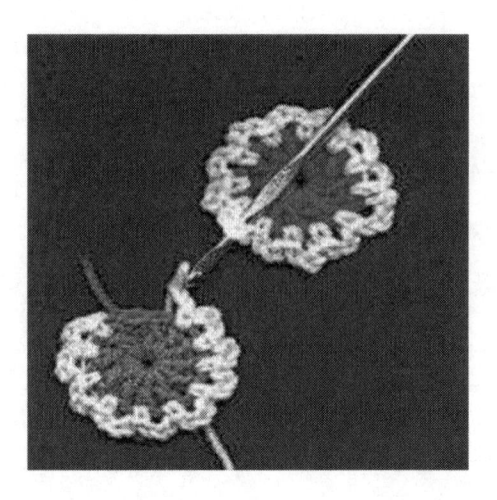

# CROCHET AFGHANS

**Step 3:** Pick up the dropped stitch and pull it through the loop, then chain 1.

**Step 4:** Single crochet in the next double crochet stitch on the second yo-yo.

**Step 5:** Chain 2, drop the stitch from your hook, then insert your hook into the next chain- 3 space on the 3rd yo-yo.

**Step 6:** Pick up dropped stitch and pull it through the loop, then chain 1.

**Step 7:** Single crochet in the next double crochet stitch on the second yo-yo, chain 3; join with a slip stitch to the first single crochet stitch on the second yo-yo, then fasten off.

**Step 8:** Link in loops 1 and 2 as completed with the second yo-yo.

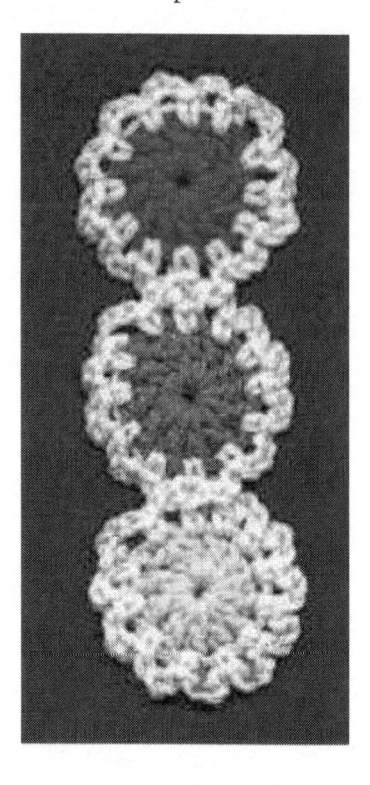

**Step 9:** Repeat all the above steps until all of the yo-yos are joined together making your afghan the length and width you desire.

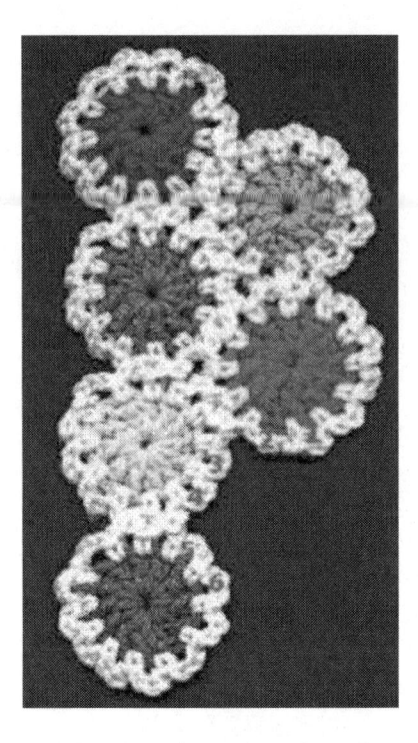

**Edging:** Using the J-10 hook and a yarn color of your choosing, work a single crochet stitch in each chain- 3 space around the yo-yos included in the afghan.

# Shell Afghan

The shell stitch is easy to master and looks beautiful. An afghan created using this stitch will look great in any room of the house.

Hook: *I-9.*

Size: *44" by 67".*

Yarn: *Worsted weight yarn in 2 colors.*

Other Materials: *Tapestry needle, scissors.*

Gauge Size: *16 stitches and 10 rows = 5 inches.*

**Pattern Instructions:**

Make a slip knot in color A and chain 133 stitches.

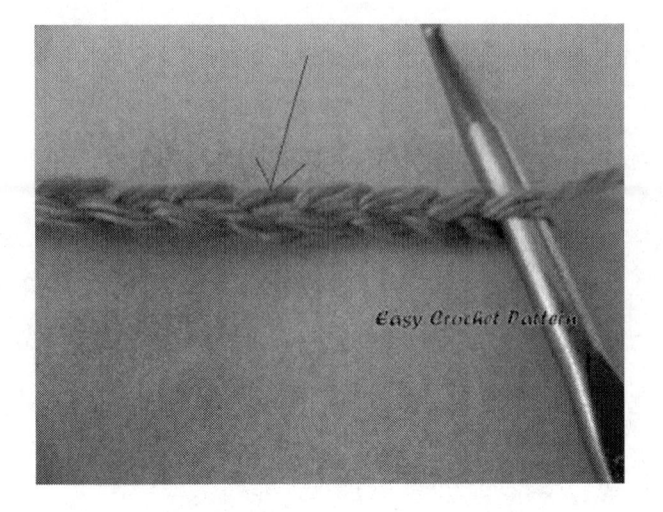

## Row 1:

- Work 2 double crochet stitches in the 4th chain from the hook.

- Skip 2 stitches, 1 single crochet, skip 2 stitches, then work 5 double crochet stitches in the next stitch – repeat this until you have 3 chains remaining.

- Skip 2 stitches, single crochet in the final chain.

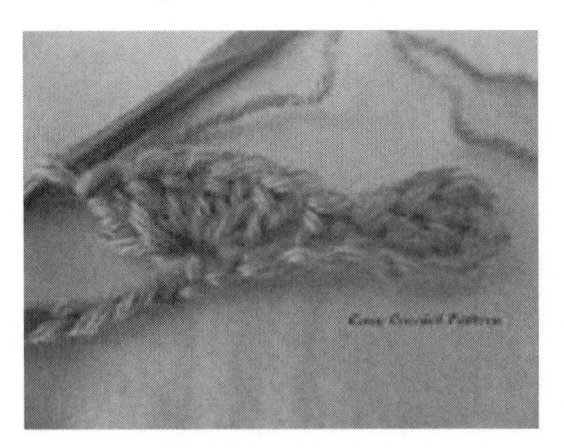

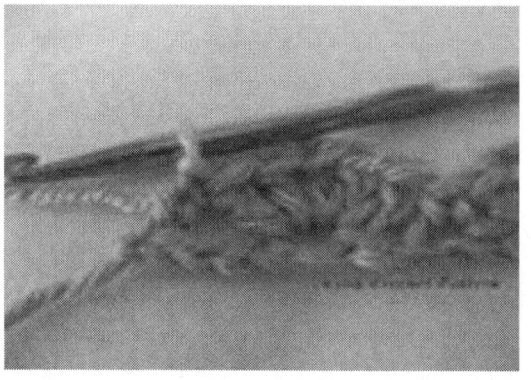

## Row 2:

- Chain 3, then turn.

- Fasten off color A and join color B with a slip stitch.

- Work 2 double crochet stitches in the single crochet stitch from the previous row.

- Skip 2 double crochet stitches, single crochet in the next stitch, skip 2 double crochet stitches, double crochet in the single crochet from the previous row – repeat this until the end of the row.

- Work a turning chain, then switch colors.

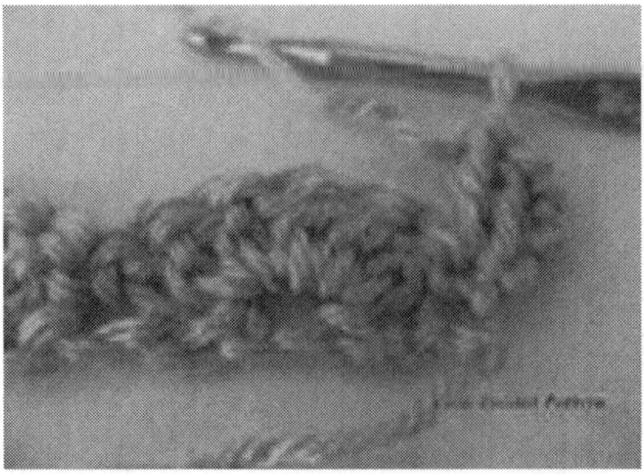

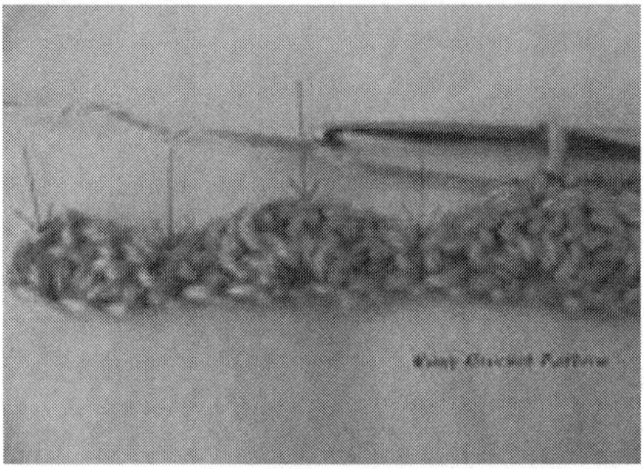

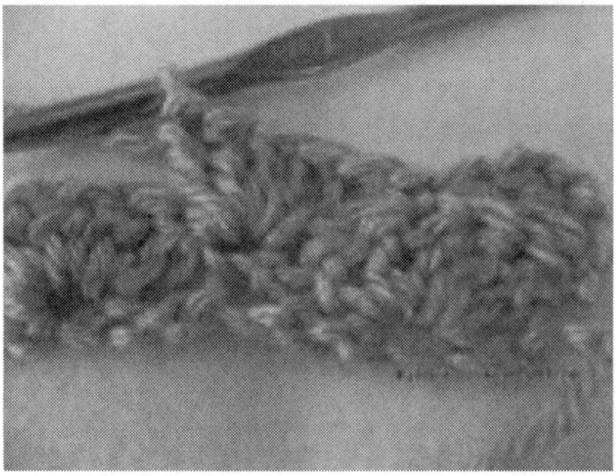

CROCHET AFGHANS

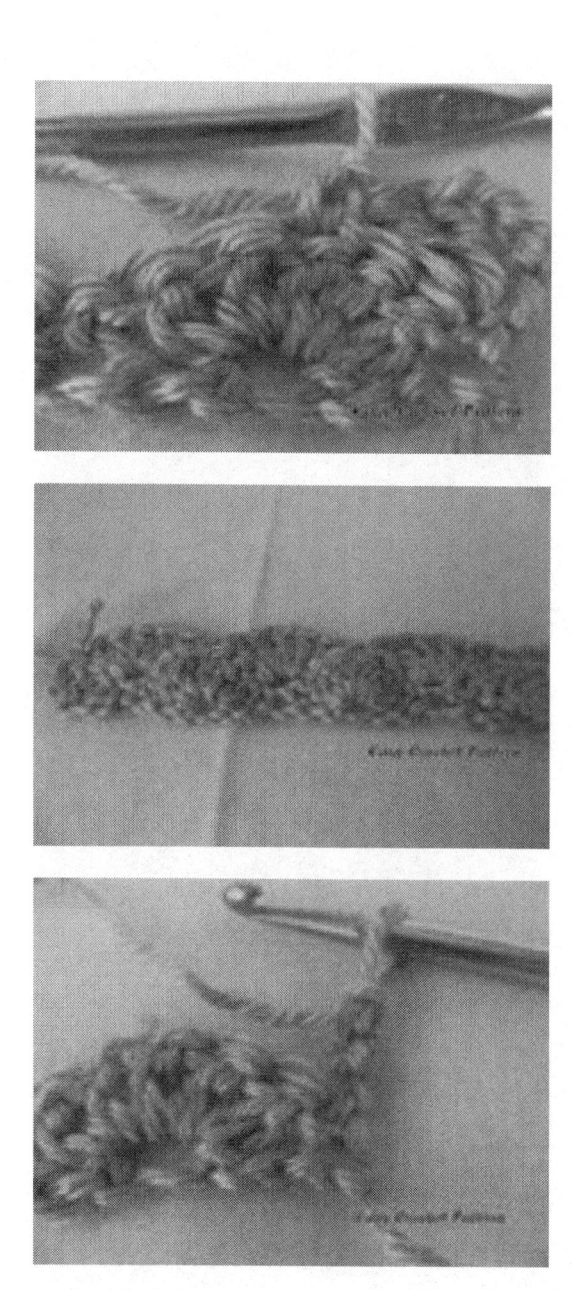

Repeat these steps until the afghan is the length you want it.

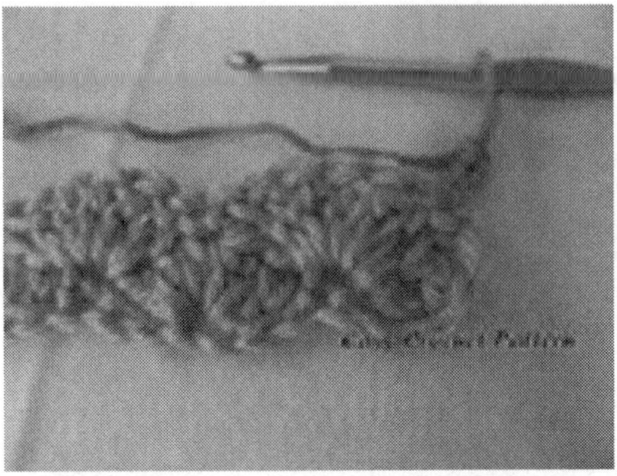

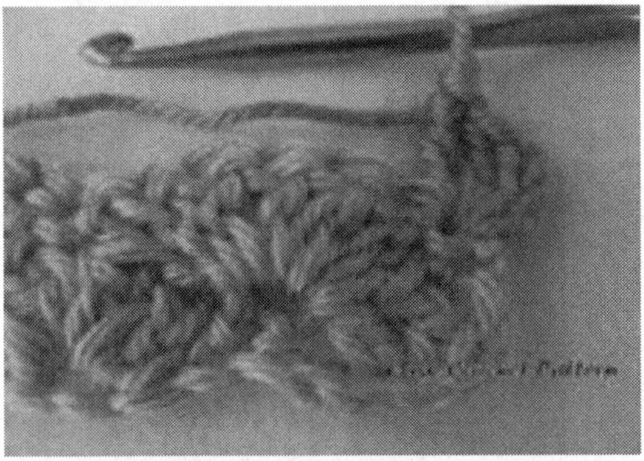

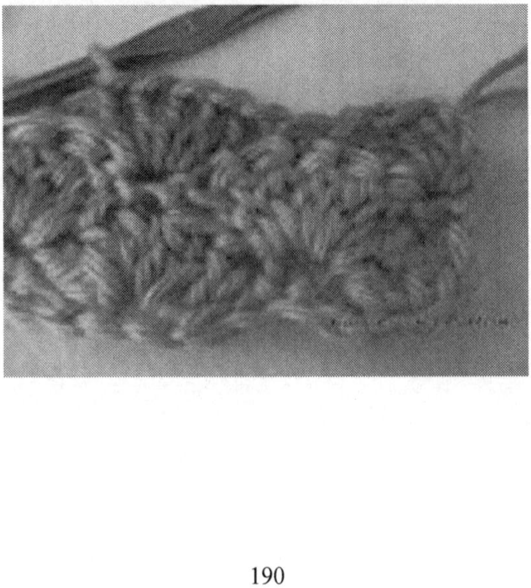

CROCHET AFGHANS

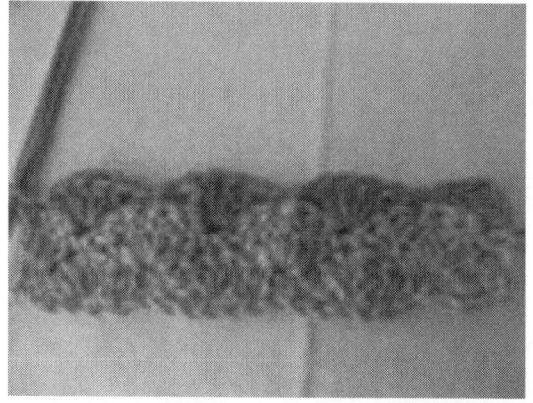

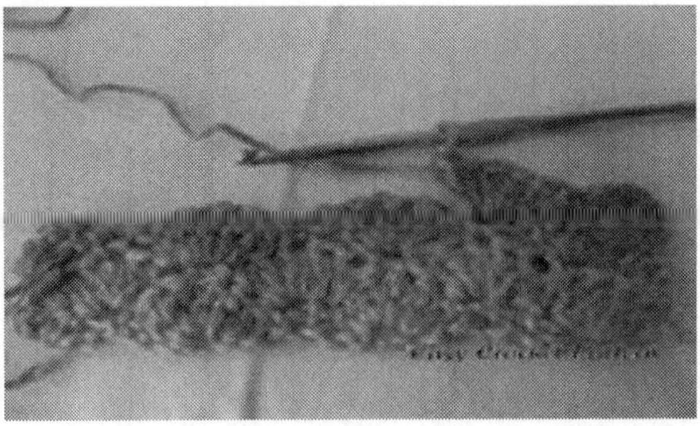

CROCHET AFGHANS

# Christmas Tree Skirt Afghan

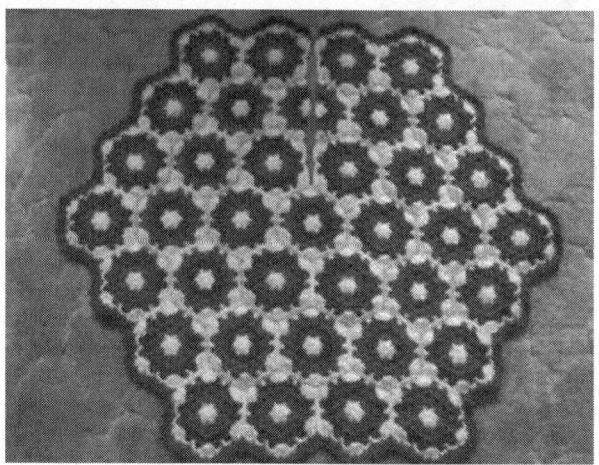

This festive design will spice up your Christmas celebrations and the complex looking design will impress all of your guests.

Blanket Size: *50" by 75"*.

Hook: *G-6, H-8 and I-9.*

Yarn: *Worsted weight acrylic in white, red and green.*

Other Materials: ***Tapestry needle, scissors.***

Gauge Size: ***24 stitches = 4 inches.***

## *Pattern Instructions:*

This pattern uses yo-yos, so the information found in the <u>Zig Zag Yo-Yo Afghan</u> section of this book will be useful to you.

### Rnd 1:

- Using white and G hook, chain 3 to form a ring.
- Chain 3.
- Work 11 double crochet stitches in the ring.
- Join in the beginning of the round.
- Chain 3.
- Fasten off.

### Rnd 2:

- With red yarn and the H hook, join using a slip stitch into any single crochet chain.
- Chain 2.
- Double crochet, chain 2, then work 2 double crochet stitches in the same space.
- Chain 1.
- Skip 1 stitch.
- Work 1 single crochet.
- 2 double crochet, chain 2, 2 double crochet in the same stitch.

- Repeat above 4 around the entire round.
- Chain 2, then fasten off.

**Rnd 3:**

- Using green yarn and the H hook, join with a slip stitch in any chain 2 space.
- Chain 2.
- Double crochet, chain 1, 2 double crochet in the same space.
- Double crochet, chain 1, double crochet in the same space.
- 2 double crochet, chain 2, 2 double crochet in the same space.
- Repeat above 2 around the entire round.
- Chain 2 and fasten off.

**Rnd 4:**

- With white yarn and I hook, join with a slip stitch in any chain 2 space.
- Chain 2.
- Work 4 double crochet stitches in the same space.
- Chain 2, single crochet in next chain, chain 2, 5 double crochet stitches in chain 2 space – repeat this around the entire round.
- Chain 2 and fasten off.

**Half Motif (Make 2)**

**Rnd 1:**

- With white yarn and G hook, chain 2 and form a ring.
- Chain 3.

- Work 6 single crochet stitches in the ring.
- Join at the top.
- Chain 3 and fasten off.

**Rnd 2:**

- With green yarn and H hook, join with a slip stitch in the first single crochet stitch.
- Chain 2.
- Work 1 double crochet stitch in the same space.
- Chain 1.
- Skip 1 stitch single crochet.
- 2 double crochet, chain 2, 2 double crochet in the next single crochet stitch.
- Repeat above 3 around entire round.
- End with 2 double crochet in the last stitch, then fasten off.

**Rnd 3:**

- With red yarn and H hook, join with a slip stitch in the first double crochet stitch.
- Chain 2.
- Work 1 double crochet in the same space.
- Double crochet, chain 1, double crochet in the same space.
- 2 double crochet, chain 2, 2 double crochet in the same space.
- Repeat above 2 around entire round.

- Finish with 2 double crochet stitches in the last stitch, then fasten off.

**Rnd 4:**

- With white yarn and I hook, join with a slip stitch in the first double crochet.

- Chain 2.

- Work 2 double crochet in the same space.

- Chain 2, single crochet in next space, chain 2, 5 double crochet in chain 2 space – repeat around entire round.

- Finish with 3 double crochet stitches in the last stitch, then fasten off.

**Joining**

Using the white yarn, whip stitch all of the motifs together in a way that suits your tastes – or by using the diagram below:

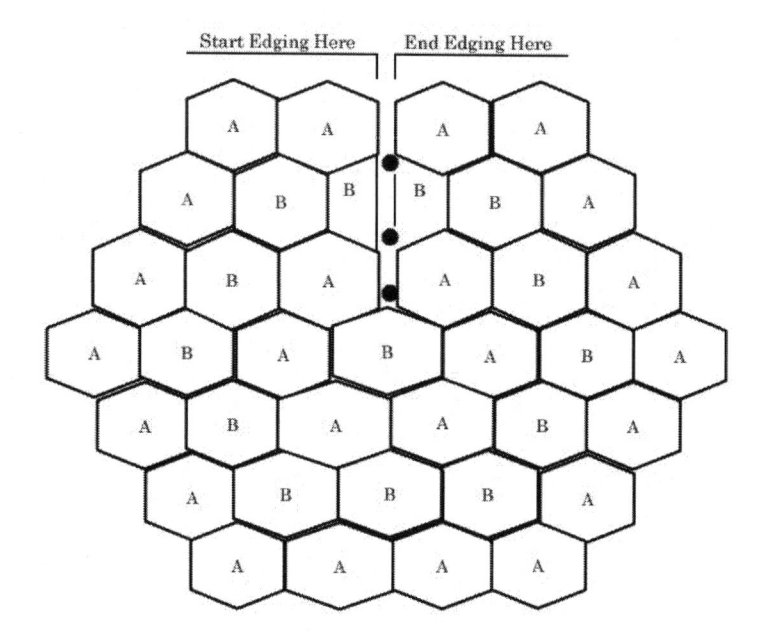

**Edging**

Once you have all the pieces attached, you may want to fix the piece together with a nice edging.

**Rnd 1:**

- With red yarn and I hook, start at the upper left-hand corner.

- Single crochet in the 3rd double crochet stitch of a 5 double crochet cluster.

- Chain 2.

- Skip 1 double crochet.

- Single crochet in the next double crochet stitch.

- Single crochet in the next single crochet stitch.

- Chain 2.

- Single crochet in the next double crochet stitch.

- Chain 2.

- Skip 1 double crochet.

- Single crochet in the next double crochet stitch.

- Chain 2.

- Single crochet in the joining stitch.

- Repeat this around, ending with a single crochet stitch in the 3rd double crochet stitch of a double crochet cluster.

- Fasten off.

**Rnd 2:**

- With green yarn and I hook starting in the upper left-hand corner.

- Single crochet, chain 2, double crochet in each chain 2 space around entire round.

- End with a single crochet stitch in the last chain 2 space and fasten off.

More Christmas patterns can be found at: thecrochetcrowd.com/christmas-july.

# Granny Stripe Afghan

This funky design uses the granny square crochet design in a new way to provide a fun pattern that everyone will love.

Hook: *I-9.*

Size: *Adult sized.*

Yarn: *Worsted weight yarn in a variety of colors.*

Other Materials: *Tapestry needle, scissors.*

Gauge Size: *4 stitches = 1 inch.*

*Pattern Instructions:*

Make a slip knot a chain 134 stitches.

**Row 1:**

- Work 1 double crochet stitch in the 2nd chain from the hook.
- Work double crochet stitches right across.

- Turn your work.

**Row 2:**

- Chain 3.

- Work 1 treble crochet stitch into the next stitch.

- Skip 2 stitches.

- Work 3 treble crochet stitches into the next stitch.

- Repeat above 2 across entire row until there are 3 stitches remaining.

- Work 2 treble crochet stitches into the last stitch on the row.

- Turn your work.

**Row 3:**

- Chain 3.

- Work 3 treble crochet stitches into the first space between the treble crochet clusters in the previous row – repeat this across the row.

- To finish, work 1 treble crochet stitch into the last stitch.

- Fasten off.

## Row 4:

- Join color B using the slip stitch.
- Chain 3 and work 1 treble crochet stitch in the same space.
- Work treble crochet stitches across the row.
- To finish, work 2 treble cluster stitches.
- Turn your work.

## Row 5:

- Chain 3.

- Work treble crochet stitches across the row.

- Fasten off.

Repeat rows 4 and 5, working 2 rows per color until the afghan is the length you desire, then fasten off.

*To find more details on Granny Stripe pattern please visit:*
*attic24.typepad.com/weblog/granny-stripe.html.*

# Easy Ripple Afghan

The ripple design looks great in a variety of colors and will look really impressive for a gift or in your own home.

Blanket Size: **_40" by 60"._**

Hook: **_I-9._**

Yarn: **_Worsted weight yarn in a variety of colors._**

Other Materials: **_Tapestry needle, scissors._**

Gauge Size: **_4 stitches = 1 inch._**

**_Pattern Instructions:_**

Make a slip knot and chain 178 stitches.

**Row 1:**

- Double crochet in the 3rd chain from the hook.

- Double crochet in the next 6 chains.

# CROCHET AFGHANS

- Work 3 double crochet stitches in the next chain.
- Double crochet in the next 6 chains.
- Work a 3 stitch decrease in the next 3 chains.
- Double crochet in the next 6 chains.
- Work 3 double crochet stitches in the next chain.
- Double crochet in the next 6 chains.
- Repeat above 4 across the row.
- Finish by working a 2 stitch decrease in the last 2 chains.
- Chain 2 and turn.

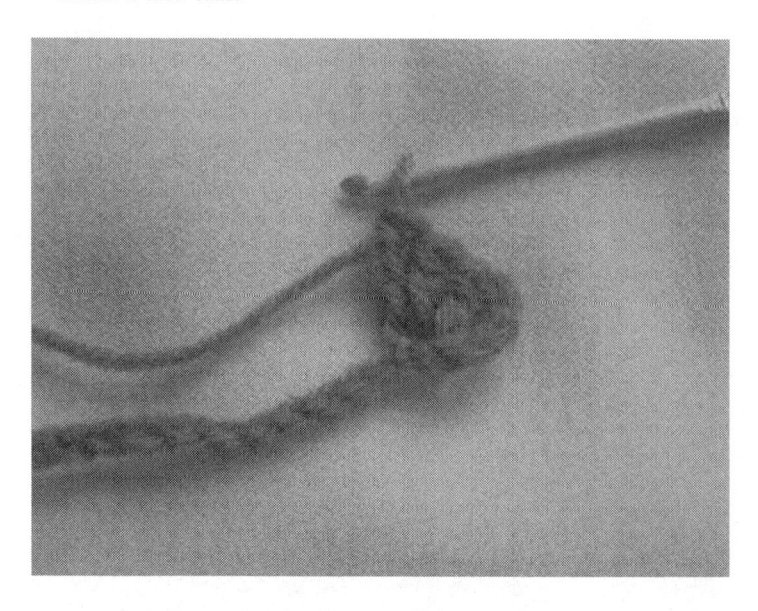

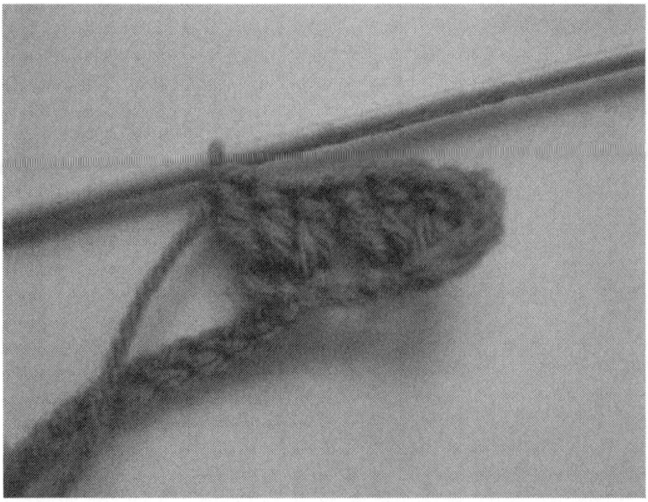

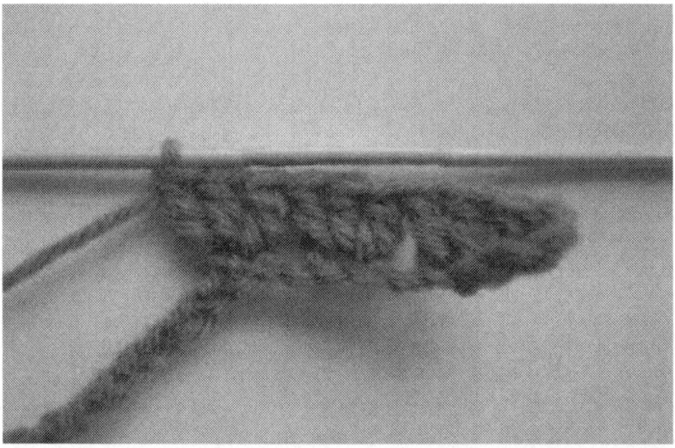

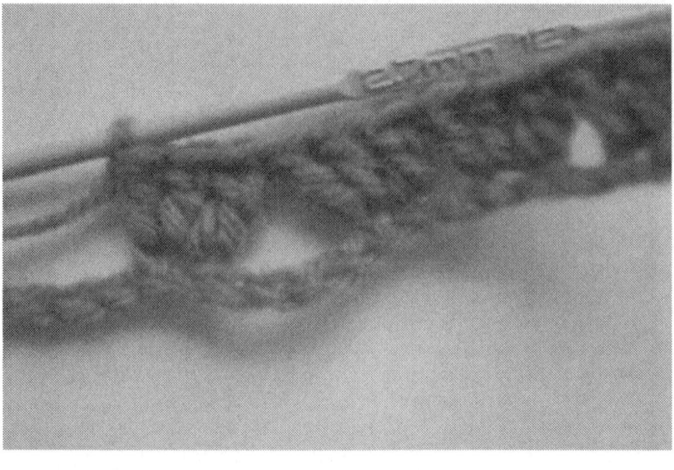

# CROCHET AFGHANS

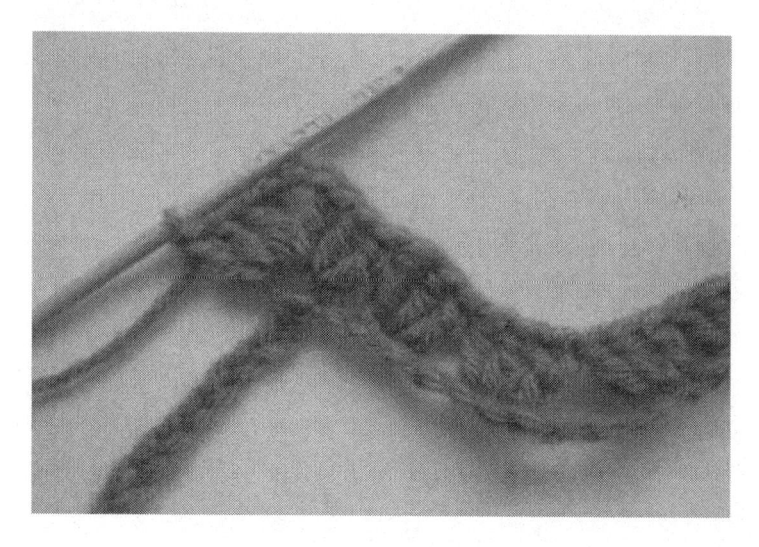

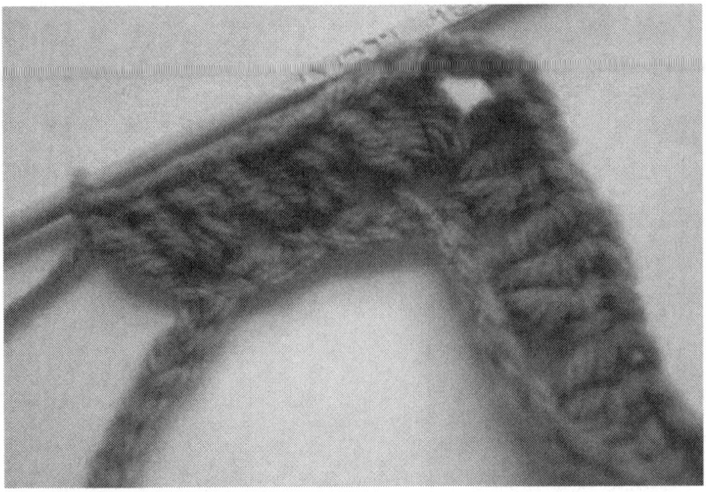

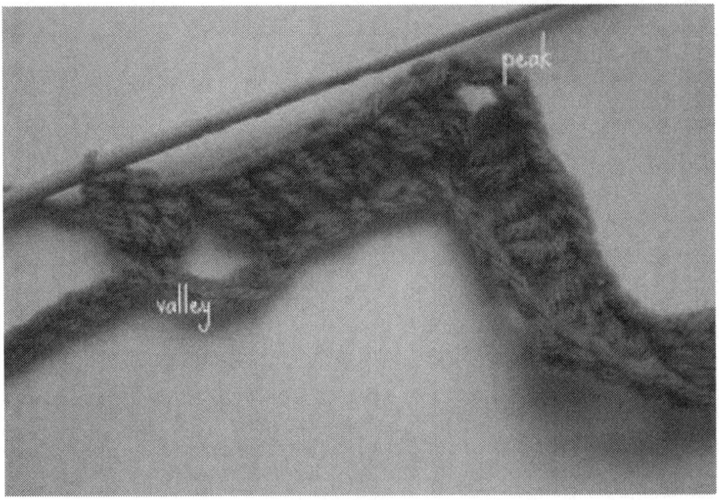
peak
valley

**Row 2:**

- Skip the first stitch.
- Double crochet in the next 7 stitches.
- Work 3 double crochet stitches in the next double crochet.
- Double crochet in the next double crochet stitches.
- Work a 3 stitch decrease in the next 3 chains.
- Double crochet in the next 6 chains.
- Work 3 double crochet stitches in the next chain.
- Double crochet in the next 6 chains.
- Repeat above 4 across the row.
- Finish by working a 2 stitch decrease in the last 2 chains.
- Chain 2 and turn.

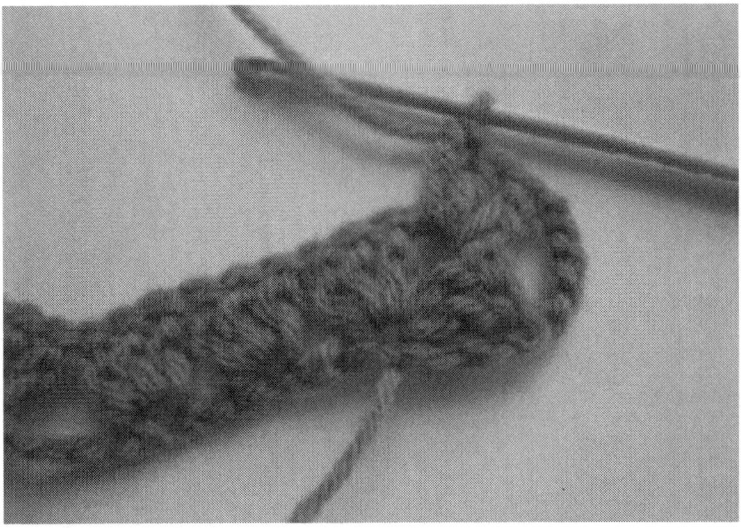

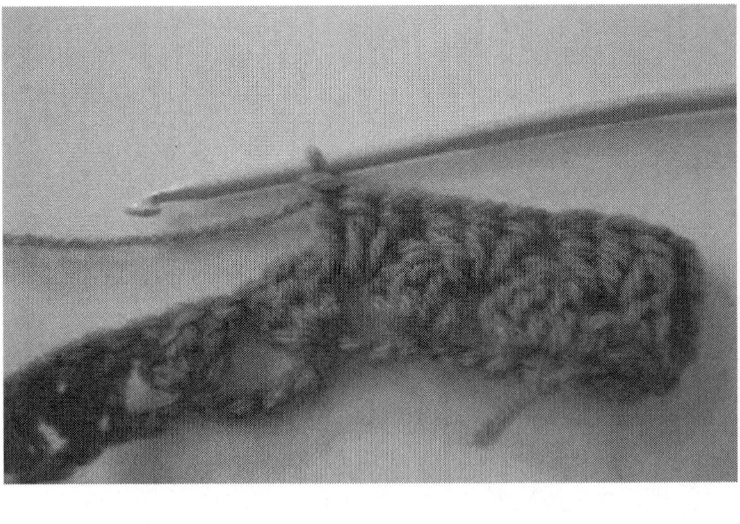

CROCHET AFGHANS

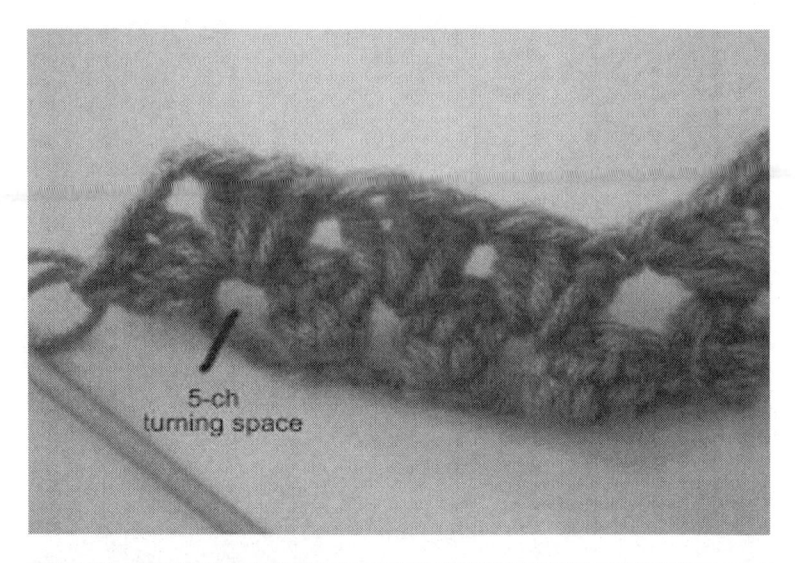

Repeat row 2 until the afghan is the desired length, changing colors as you like, then fasten off.

# CROCHET AFGHANS

# Ripple Afghans

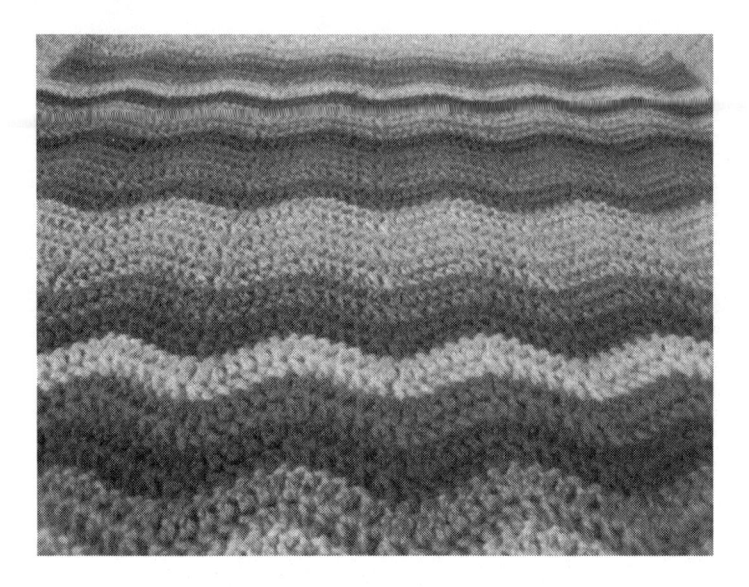

This pattern uses the straightforward ripple stitch, but the end result is just as eye-catching and striking.

Hook: **K-10**.

Size: **47 by 60"**.

Yarn: **54 ounces of worsted weight yarn in 6+ colors**.

Other Materials: **Tapestry needle, scissors**.

Gauge Size: **11 double crochet = 4 inches.**

**Pattern Instructions:**

With color A, make a slip knot and chain 131 stitches.

CROCHET AFGHANS

**Row 1:**

- Double crochet in 5th chain from hook.

- Double crochet in next 10 chains.

- Double crochet, chain 1, then double crochet in next chain.

- Double crochet in next 11 chains.

- Skip next 2 chains.

- Double crochet in next 11 chains.

- Double crochet, chain 1, double crochet in next chain.

- Double crochet in next 11 chains.

- Skip next 2 chains.

- Repeat above 5 instructions 4 times, ending the 4th time with – skip next chain, double crochet in the last chain and turn.

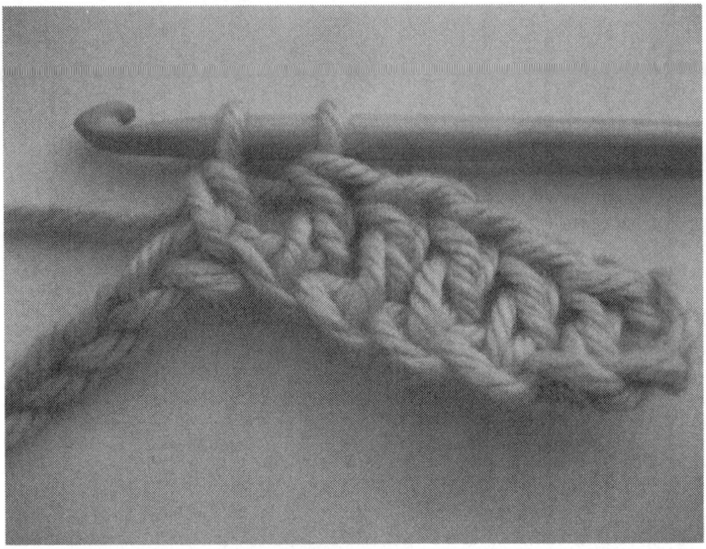

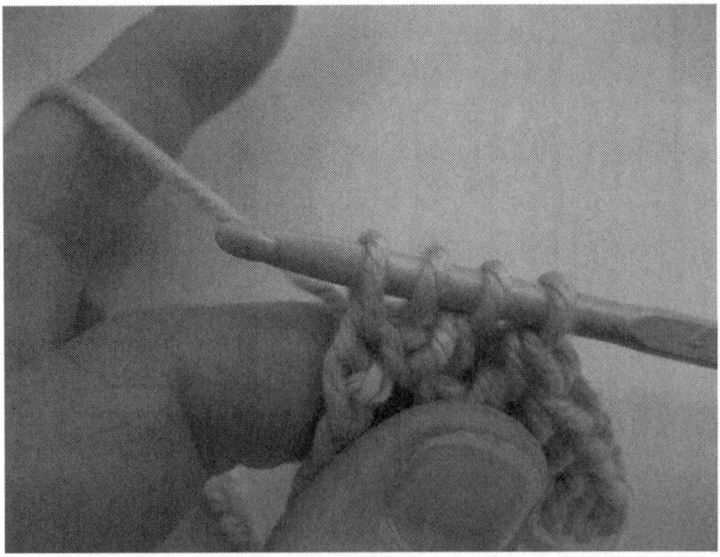

CROCHET AFGHANS

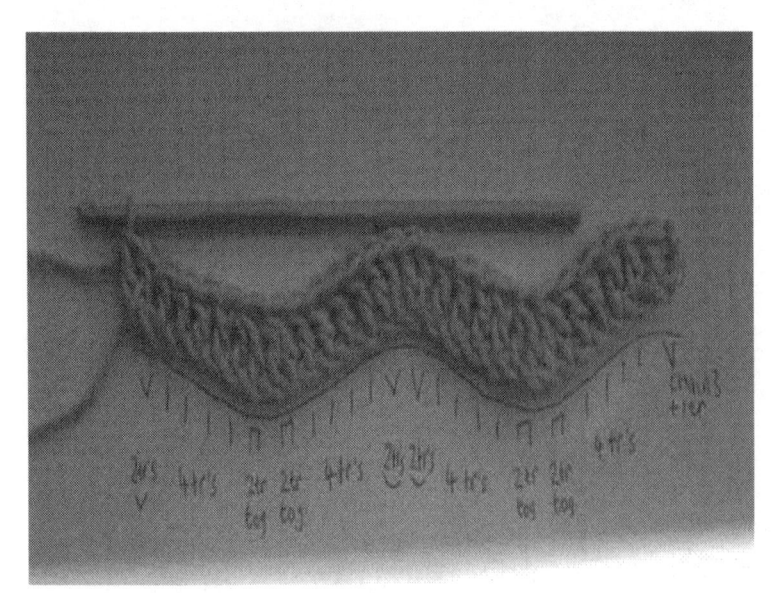

**Row 2:**

- Chain 3.

- Skip first 2 double crochet stitches.

- Double crochet in next 11 double crochet stitches.

- Double crochet, chain 1, double crochet in next chain- 1 space.

- Double crochet in next 11 double crochet stitches.

- Skip next 2 double crochet stitches.

- Repeat above 4 instructions 5 times, ending the 5th time with – skip 1 double crochet, then double crochet in the beginning chain- 3.

- Turn your work.

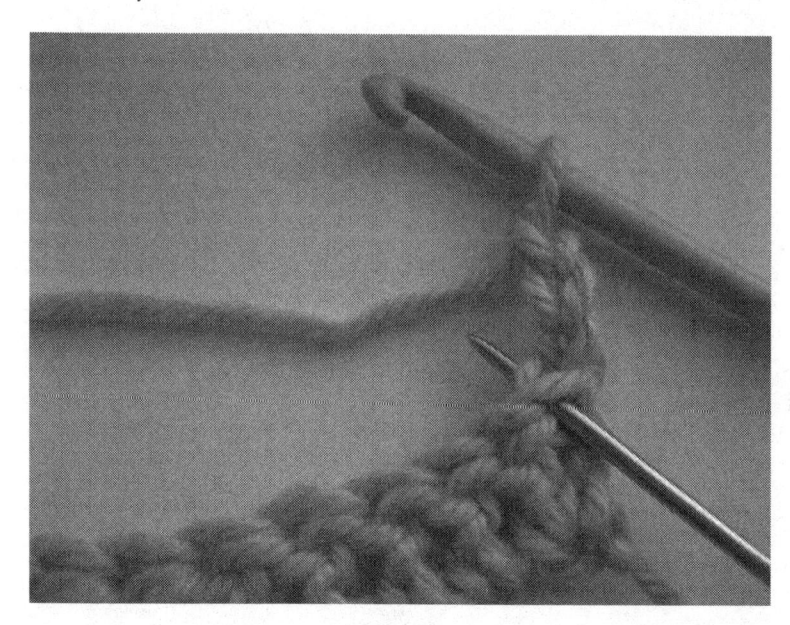

EMMA BROWN

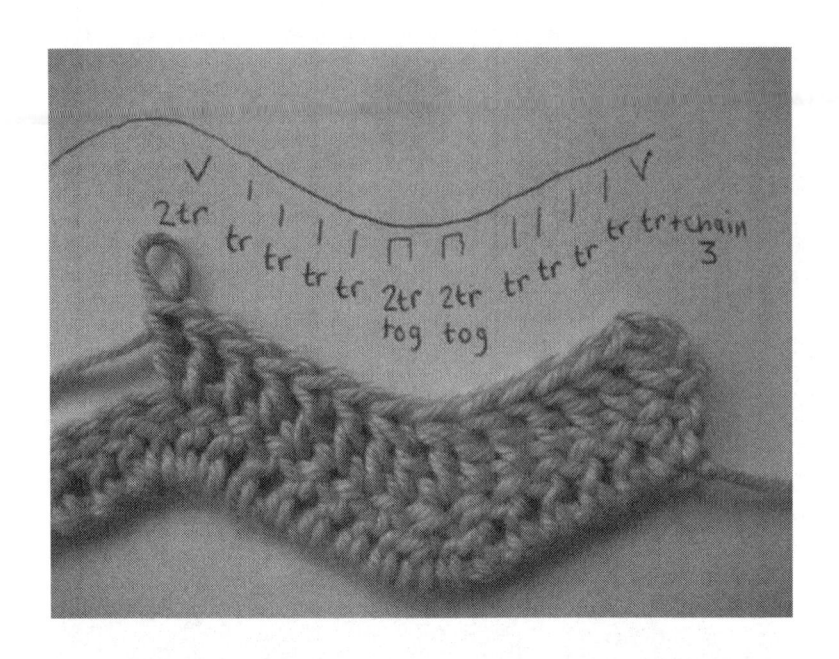

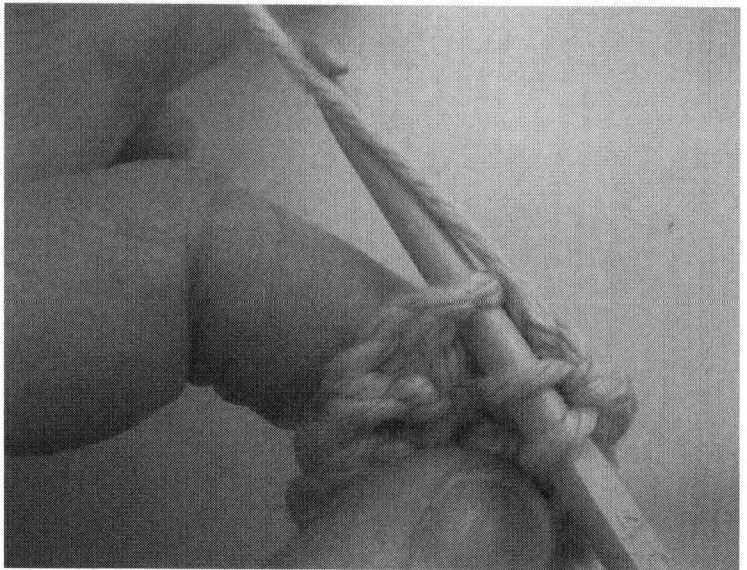

**Rows 3-38:** Repeat Row 2 in the following color sequence: 3 rows in color A, 5 rows in color C, 5 rows in color B, 5 rows in color D, 5 rows in color E, 5 rows in color F, 2 rows in color A, 2 rows in color C, 2 rows in color B, and 2 rows in color D, changing to color E in last stitch.

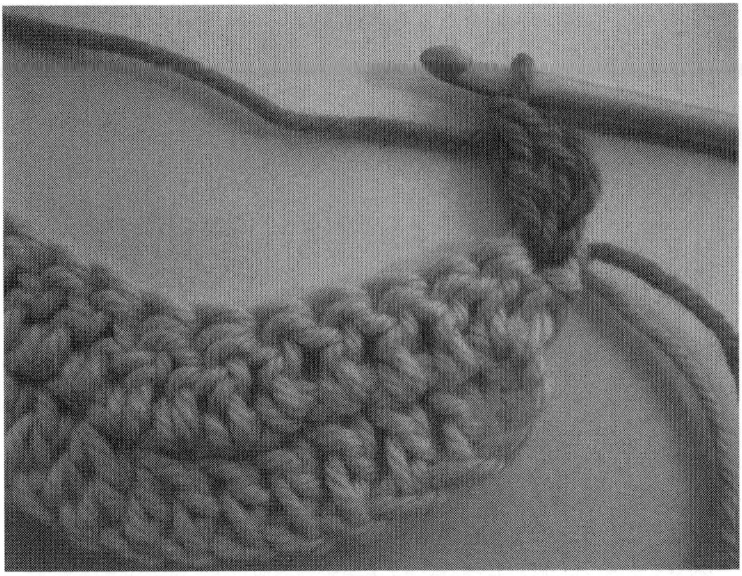

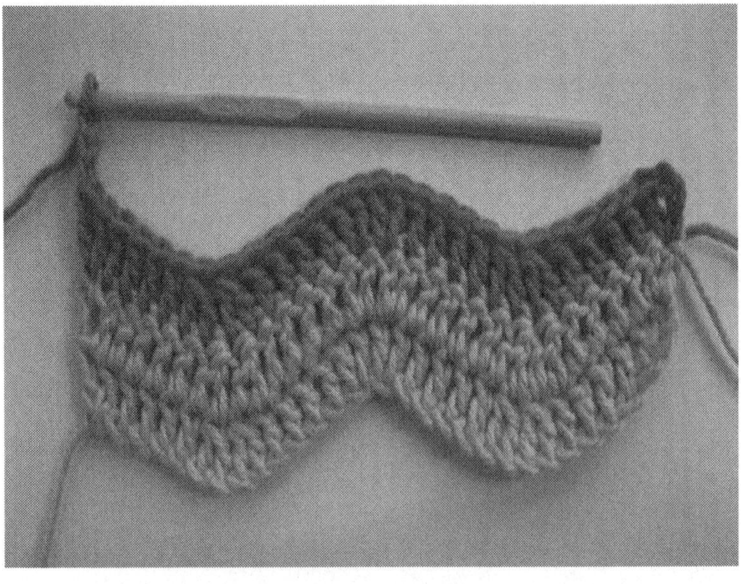

**Row 39:**

- With color E, chain 2.

- Skip first 2 double crochet stitches.

- Half-double crochet in the next 11 double crochet stitches.

- Half-double crochet, chain 1, half-double crochet in next chain- 1 space.

- Half-double crochet in next 11 double crochet stitches.

- Skip the next 2 double crochet stitches.

Repeat above 5 instructions 5 times, ending the 5th time with – skip 1 double crochet, half-double crochet in beginning chain- 3.

**Rows 40-43:** Repeat Row 39 in the following color sequence: 1 row in color F, 1 row in color E, 1 row in color F, 1 row in color E, changing to color D in last stitch.

**Rows 44-81:** Repeat Row 2 in the following color sequence: 2 rows in color D, 2 rows color B, 2 rows color C, 2 rows color A, 5 rows color F, 5 rows color E, 5 rows color D, 5 rows color B, 5 rows color C, and 5 rows color A. Fasten off.

*To find more details on Ripple Afghans please visit www.leisurearts.com/5950*

# Granny Square Crochet Pillow

Although this pattern is technically not for an afghan, it's nice to know how to create a pillow to go with the blanket you've made. This pattern isn't too complicated so with your crocheting knowledge obtained in this guide, you won't have any trouble with it.

Hook: **H-8**.

Size: **50x50cm**.

Yarn: **Worsted weight yarn in 3 colors.**

Other Materials: **Tapestry needle, scissors, pillow stuffing.**

Gauge Size: **3 double crochet stitches = 1 inch.**

*Pattern Instructions:*

**Step 1:** With color A, make a ring and secure with a stitch.

**Step 2:**

- Chain 2.

- Work 2 double crochet stitches in the ring.

- Chain 1.

- Work 3 double crochet stitches in the ring.

- Continue until you have 4 Granny Clusters (3 double crochet stitches in the next chain, then chain 1).

CROCHET AFGHANS

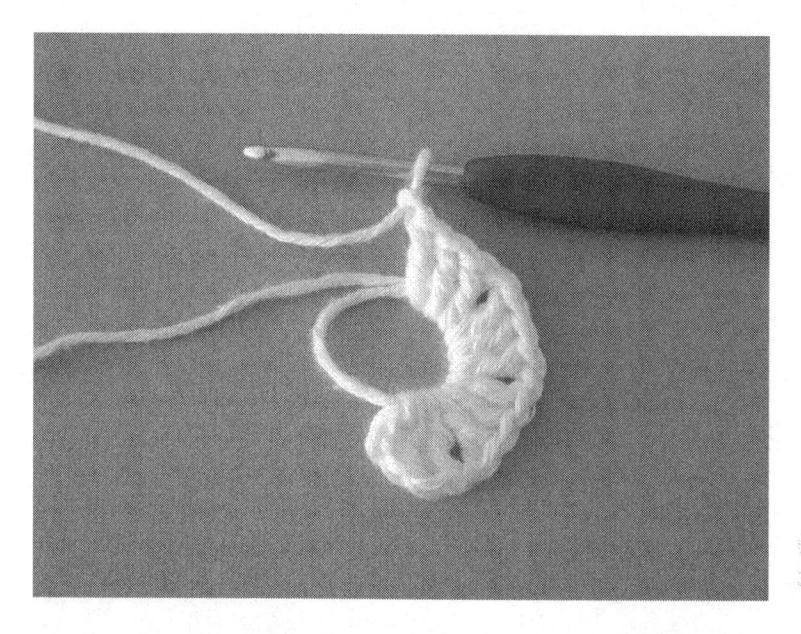

**Step 3:** Cut the yarn and pull your loop through a hook. Pull the ring closed. You'll see a circle forming.

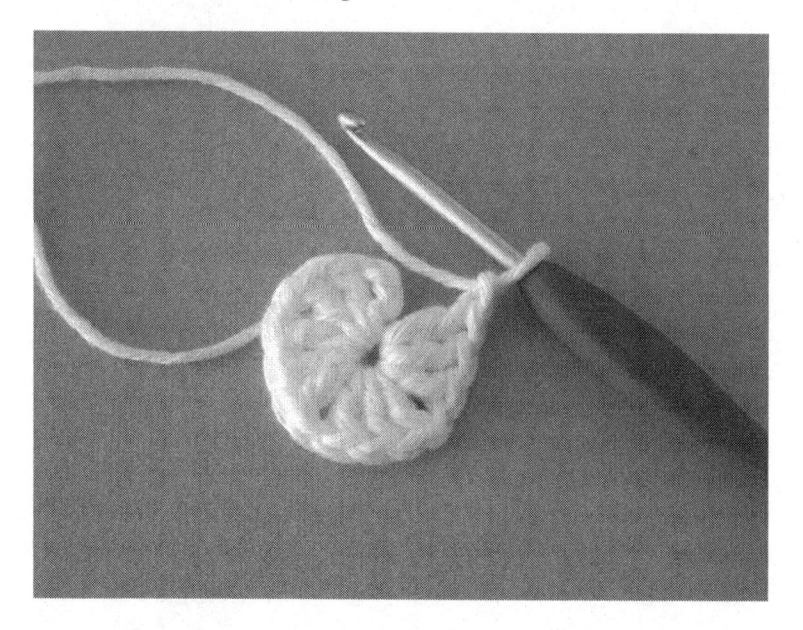

**Step 4:** Thread the end of your yarn through your tapestry needle and insert it from front to back in the first double crochet stitch you made, skipping the initial 2 chains.

**Step 5:** Pull through, then insert your needle from front to back through the back loop of the first stitch you made.

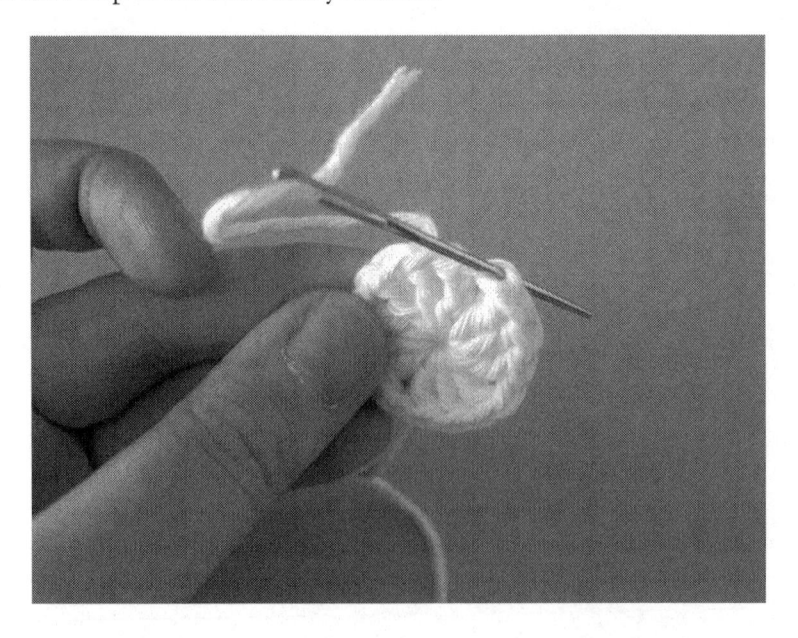

**Step 6:** Pull tight and sew in the end. Leave the other yarn end for now.

# CROCHET AFGHANS

**Step 7:** With color B, make a slip knot.

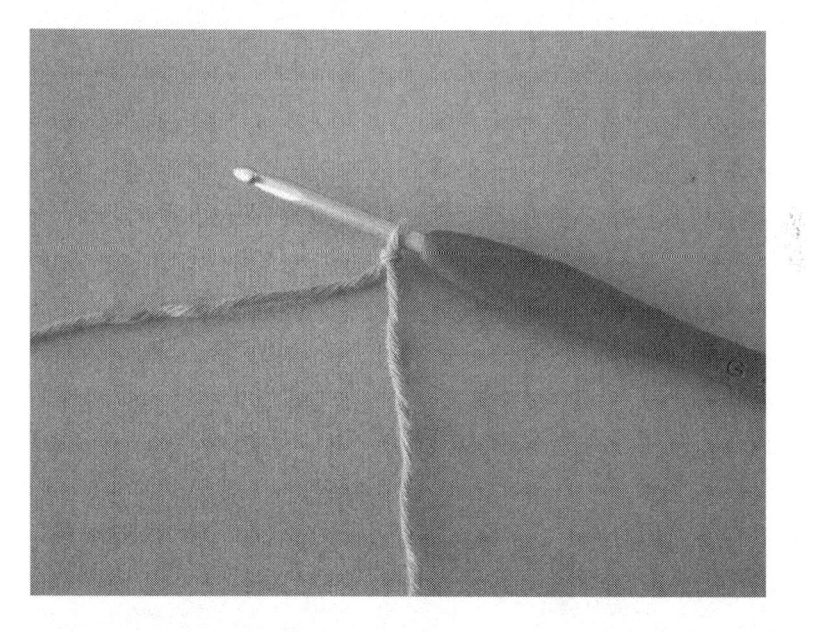

**Step 8:** Crochet 1 Granny Cluster, chain 1, then crochet another Granny Cluster.

**Step 9:** Repeat this in all 4 corners. Your piece will now start to look like a square.

**Step 10:** Finish using steps 4 to 6 with your tapestry needle. Also sew in the yarn end left over from step 6.

CROCHET AFGHANS

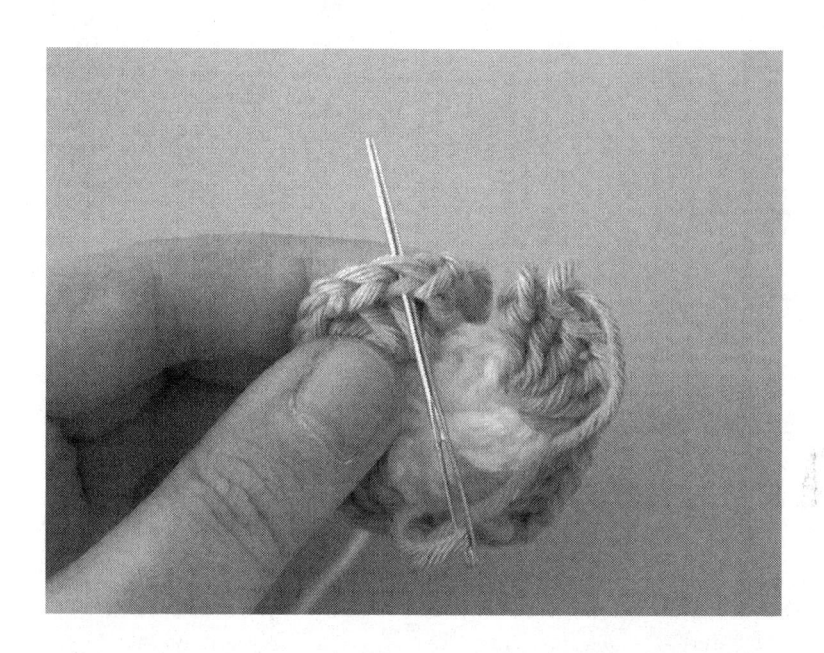

**Step 11:** With color C, make a slip knot. Starting in the middle of one side, work a Granny Cluster. When you get to the corner, work 2 Granny Clusters separated by 1 chain.

**Step 12:** Repeat around the round, and finish off using steps 4 to 6.

CROCHET AFGHANS

**Step 13:** With color A, work Granny Clusters in the spaces between the clusters of the previous round. Be sure to work 2 Granny Clusters separated by 1 chain in the corners. Finish off using steps 4 to 6.

**Step 14:** Using steps 1 – 13, make 24 more Granny Squares.

**Step 15:** Now it's time to join the squares. Work from left to right, grab 2 squares and press the 'right sides' together.

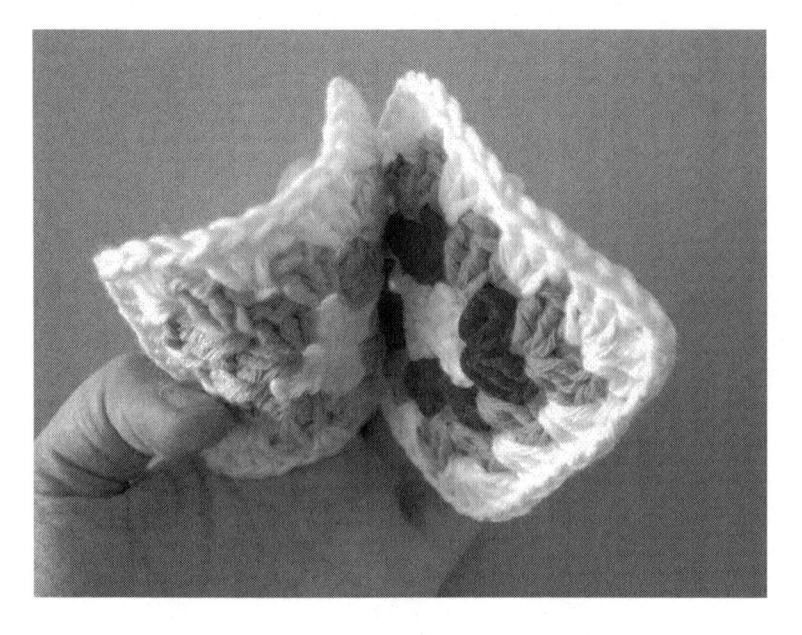

CROCHET AFGHANS

**Step 16:** Insert your hook into the corner stitch of both squares, using back loops only.

**Step 17:** Slip stitch the squares together. Pull the yarn through both loops and the loop on your hook. Work until you reach the corner on both squares and grab 2 more squares. Continue to join the squares in this way.

**Step 18:** Once the squares are sewn together, Granny Cluster around the edge. Be sure to work 2 Granny Clusters separated by 1 chain in the corners.

**Step 19:** For the back portion of the cushion, make a large granny square. You can use steps 1 to 13 and keep expanding.

**Step 20:** To join the front and back pieces, start by placing them 'wrong sides' together.

**Step 21:** Slip stitch the pieces together, using the inner loops.

**Step 22:** When you get to a corner, make a single crochet stitch, chain 1 then make another single crochet stitch in the same stitch.

**Step 23:** When you have 3 sides joined, insert a pillow.

CROCHET AFGHANS

**Step 24:** Crochet the final side together and fasten off.

# Advanced

## Aran Crochet Afghan

The stitches needed to complete this afghan are very complex and should only be completed by crocheters with a lot of experience. Once you have practiced a few of the intermediate patterns given in this guide, you may wish to try this one.

Hook: **N-15.**

Hook: **48" by 62".**

Yarn: **9 – 10 skeins of chunky yarn.**

Other Materials: **Tapestry needle, scissors.**

Gauge Size: **4 stitches = 1 inch.**

### Pattern Instructions:

Make a slip knot and chain 101 stitches.

**Row 1:** Single crochet in the 2nd chain from hook and in every chain across.

**Row 2:** Single crochet in every single crochet across.

**Row 3:**

- Single crochet in the first single crochet.
- Chain 3, skip next single crochet, single crochet in each of the 3 chains – repeat across the row.
- Single crochet in the last single crochet.
- Chain 1.

**Rows 4-5:** Repeat row 2.

**Row 6:** Single crochet in the first single crochet across, then chain 1.

## *Edging:*

**Row 1:** Do not turn your work; then single crochet across the sides of rows 1 to 6 at one end of the afghan, turn and fasten off.

*More information on Aran Hearts crochet pattern can be found at: redheart.com/free-patterns/aran-hearts-throw*

# GLOSSARY

Crochet patterns will often use abbreviations to make the instructions more concise.

**Below is a list of the most common.**

*[ ]* - Work instructions within the brackets as many times as directed.

*( )* - Work instructions within the parentheses as many times as directed.

\* - Repeat the instructions following the single asterisk as directed.

\* \* - Repeat the instructions between asterisks as many times as directed.

" - Inches.

*alt* - Alternate.

*approx* - Approximately.

*beg* - Begin.

*bet* - Between.

*BL* - Back Loops.

*bo* - Bobble.

*BP* - Back Post.

*BPdc* - Back Post Double Crochet.

*BPsc* - Back Post Single Crochet.

*BPtr* - Back Post Treble Crochet.

*CA* - Color A.

*CB* - Color B.

*CC* - Contrasting Color.

*ch* - Chain Stitch.

*ch-* - Refers to chain or space previously made.

*ch-sp* - Chain space.

*CL* - Cluster.

*Cm* - Centimeters.

*Cont* - Continue.

*Dc* - Double Crochet.

*dc2tog* - Double crochet 2 stitches together.

*Dec* - Decrease.

*Dtr* - Double treble.

*FL* - Front Loops.

*FO* - Finished Object.

*Foll* - Follow.

*FP* - Front Post.

*FPdc* - Front Post Double Crochet.

*FPsc* - Front Post Single Crochet.

*FPtr* - Front Post Treble Crochet.

*G* - Gram.

*Hdc* - Half Double Crochet.

*Inc* - Increase.

*lp(s)* - Loop(s).

*M* - Meters.

*MC* - Main Color.

*Mm* - Millimeters.

*Oz* - Ounces.

*P* - Picot.

*pat(s)* or *patt* - Pattern(s).

*Pc* - Popcorn.

*Pm* - Place Maker.

*Prev* - Previous.

*Rem* - Remain.

*Rep* - Repeat.

*rnd(s)* - Round(s).

*RS* - Right Side.

*Sc* - Single Crochet.

*sc2tog* - Single crochet 2 stitches together.

*Sk* - Skip.

*Sl st* - Slip Stitch.

*sp(s)* - Space(s).

*st(s)* - Stitches.

*tch* or *t-ch* - Turning Chain.

*Tbl* - Through Back Loop.

*Tog* - Together.

*Tr* - Treble Crochet.

*Trtr* - Triple Treble Crochet.

*UFO* - Unfinished Object.

*WIP* - Work in Progress.

*WS* - Wrong Side.

*yd(s)* - Yard(s).

*yo* - Yarn Over.

*Yoh* - Yarn Over Hook.

# FAQ

### - What is a good yarn for making a crochet afghan?

The pattern will tell you which yarn is most suited to the stitches it suggests, but if you want to create your own pattern, *worsted acrylic* is the most common. Check out the yarn section of this guide for more information.

### - How to start my ripple crochet afghan?

There are many brilliant online resources for crocheting and patterns, and YouTube is brilliant for user tips, tricks and advice. There is a selection of ripple afghan patterns included in this guide.

### - How hard is it to crochet Afghan blankets as a beginner?

The majority of crochet afghan patterns are aimed at beginners, which means that with even the most basic crochet knowledge, you should have no trouble completing a pattern.

### - Where can I find some Western crochet afghan patterns?

The Internet is filled with all sorts of crochet afghan patterns. There are many free ones available at sites such as:
*crochetpatterncentral.com/directory/afghans.php*.

There is a wonderful selection of Western crochet afghan patterns at:
*superlativestitchery.com/indianwesterncrochet.html*.

### - How do you safely store crocheted afghans?

There are many ways you can store your crocheted afghans – whether it's while they are still a work in progress or when they're finished. This includes:

- *Ziplock bags* – Which are see-through and are available in a range of sizes so you can use them for any project.

- *Tote bags* – These are great for carrying your afghans around, especially if they are work-in-progress and you want to crochet on the move.

- *Plastic shoeboxes* – If you aren't concerned with portability, this is a great way to keep them tidy.

- *Yarn bags* – You are already buying the yarn, why not use the bag productively?

- *Specialist boxes/bags* – You could even buy (or make!) yourself something special to keep all of your crocheting stuff together.

### - How do you make a crocheted afghan pillow?

You may wish to crochet a pillow to match your afghan. There is an example pattern for this in this guide.

### - What yarn requirements are there to crochet a baby afghan?

When it comes to crocheting an afghan for a baby, you will want to ensure that it is the right weight and feel for them. You will want to think about using a lighter weight and a woolen yarn to make sure the baby is kept warm. *Vanna's Choice by Lion Brand* is recommended on many parenting formats.

### - Can you use a plastic canvas pattern to crochet an afghan?

A plastic canvas is a lightweight material with regularly spaced holes, used for the foundation for craft work. You can use one to crochet anything, including afghans. A list of patterns that use a plastic canvas can be found at *freepatterns.com/list.html?cat_id=8*.

### - How much yarn is needed for a crocheted granny square afghan?

The pattern for the granny square afghan will let you know how much yarn you will need according to what size you want it. A granny square afghan

CROCHET AFGHANS

will require more yarn than a straight afghan pattern due to its complexity.

### - What are some nice color combinations for crocheted afghans?

When considering what color combinations you want to use for your afghan, you need to think about what you – or whoever the afghan is for – likes and what will go with the rest of their furniture. You don't want to use more than five colors as it can start to look messy, and the chart below gives a good indicator of what colors look good together:

**MIXED COLOR BAGS**

Bags of 10 (2 balls / 5 colors) for Extra Fine, Medium, Boucle, and Brushed Mohair:

**Nemo's World**
Mauve
Lime
Turquoise
Baby Blue
Pale Turquoise

**Rainy Day**
Tobacco
Charcoal
Eau de Nil
Dark Blue Plum
Dark Denim

**Camouflage**
Avocado
Dark Khaki Green
Khaki
Olive Green
Khaki Olive

**Pebble Beach**
Camel
Sand
Light Grey
Eau de Nil or Sage
Light Denim

**Smoke**
Charcoal
Denim
Dark Grey
Light Denim
Aubergine

**Herbs and Spices**
Buttercup
Pale Mauve
Pale Rust
Grass Green
Pistachio

**Wild Berries**
Burgundy
Dark Blue Plum
Fuchsia
Aubergine
Amethyst

**Sage**
Camel
Sage
Sand
Eau de Nil
Linen

**Cappuccino**
Charcoal Brown
Dark Brick
Sand
Chocolate
Camel

**Underwater**
Navy
Lichen
Sea Green
Deep Turquoise
Pale Green

**Strawberry Shortcake**
Sand
Peach
Dusky Pink
Camel
Baby Pink

**Highland Heather**
Amethyst
Pale Jacaranda
Heather
Jacaranda
Pale Mauve or Mauve

251

| Tuscan Terracotta | Shakespeare | Shifting Sands | Rosewood |
|---|---|---|---|
| Dark Rust | Aubergine | Dark Camel | Dark Brick |
| Rust | Dark Blue Plum | Natural | Burgundy |
| Pale Rust | Pineview | Linen | Rose |
| Tobacco | Tomato | Sand | Burnt Red |
| Dark Brick | Green Potion | Oyster | Mahogany |

| Perfect Pinks | Autumn Avenue | Desert Moon | Dana's Choice |
|---|---|---|---|
| Bright Pink | Copper | Dark Camel | Mink |
| Hyacinth | Burnt Orange | Aubergine | Dark Camel |
| Baby Pink | Pale Rust | Jacaranda | Charcoal Brown |
| Heather | Wheat | Copper | Dark Grey |
| Fuchsia | Avocado | Sunshine | Rose |

| Bollywood | Forest Fruits | By the Beach | Tudor Rose |
|---|---|---|---|
| Fuchsia | Amethyst | Saffron | Light Grey |
| Orange | Green Potion | Pale Green | Sage or Eau de Nil |
| Red | Dark Blue Plum | Natural | Pale Amethyst |
| Acid Green | Lichen | Heather | Denim |
| Royal Blue | Dark Turquoise | Acid Green | Dusky Pink |

*substitutions may occur*  **Lemonade :** Sunshine, Lemon, Acid Yellow, Lime Green, Acid Green

### - Is there a way to divide a crocheted afghan?

If you crochet an afghan that is too big, you may wish to cut it and divide it into separate pieces. Cutting crochet fabric may seem daunting, but it is possible, as long as you do the preparatory work. As long as you bind the area that has been cut, the afghan won't fall apart. There is a section about <u>finishing off crochet</u> in this guide.

### - What kind of stitch is best for crocheting an afghan?

Crocheting an afghan usually primarily involves single crochet stitches, double crochet stitches or afghan stitches. Which of these you should use depends on what you want the afghan to look like. The pattern will tell you what it uses.

# CONCLUSION

So as you can see from this guide, crocheting is a skill that is easy to pick up, and fun to master. Once you have gotten to grips with the basic stitches and techniques, working out afghan patterns will quickly become natural and then you go on to add your own personalized touches to the designs.

Crocheting is a brilliant way to create unique, homemade gifts, with a personal touch, or even cute little additions to spice up your own home. There isn't a better feeling than creating something yourself, and seeing others admire it! What better way to greet a new baby into the world than to give an afghan created by your own hands, making a practical gift very special?

There are many amazing resources online for crocheters – in fact, there is quite a huge community of web pages and forums where users can share their tips and tricks. This is a great way to discover more about your new skill, whilst meeting new people from all over the world and making friends. Once you have the ability to crochet, you won't look back!

# ABOUT THE AUTHOR

Emma Brown learned to crochet at her grandmother's feet. There were many summers that she and her parents stayed with their grandparents for weeks, and every day, Emma would sit beside her grandmother, untangling her yarn and learning how to crochet–first, a little hat for her stuffed dog, and then one for her father, and by the age of ten, she was crocheting full-size afghans as Christmas presents for her family.

The older Emma got, the more about crocheting she learned, making it a point to find the most complicated and tedious patterns she could and bringing them to her grandmother during the summer. Together they would figure them out, and then, soon, Emma did not need her grandmother's help with the patterns any more, and they could just sit side by side and crochet.

Emma Brown's knowledge of crocheting is more extensive than most and was built by trial and error–so she knows what really works for someone who is first starting to learn or who wants to progress from the basics to more advanced patterns and techniques. She has started crocheting circle in just about every city she's lived in, passing her knowledge on to others, before deciding to write a book that would encompass the entirety of experience and expertise.

Made in the USA
San Bernardino, CA
24 February 2019